*This book is dedicated to the human spirit,
and to all who embrace change as a means
of exploration, fulfillment and adventure.*

JUST GO!

LEAVE THE TREADMILL
FOR A WORLD OF ADVENTURE

SKIP & GABI YETTER

JUST GO!

LEAVE THE TREADMILL
FOR A WORLD OF ADVENTURE

SKIP & GABI YETTER

©2015 THE MEANDERTHALS PUBLISHING

ISBN 978-0-9962370-0-0

Table of Contents

Editor's Note 1
Preface.. 5
Introduction... 7
Identifying the Disease 17
Researching and Soul Searching 39
Practical Matters 53
Making the Break.. 63
Moving: From Here to There 71
Contrasts: Then and Now 87
Adapting to Change 109
Healthcare.. 125
Money Matters... 143
Personal Security 149
A Shift in Thinking/Lessons Learned 155
What Now? 163
Section II: Stories from the Other Side of Convention 171
I'm Young and Fancy Free 177
Hitting 30 and Open To Change................................ 191
Experienced and Keen to Explore 211
Midlife and the World is My Oyster........................... 223
Midlife and Beyond.. 237
Just the Two of Us 241
And The Family Came Too 251
All The Way Outside the Box..................................... 271
What Does it Cost? 275
Resources 287
Acknowledgements... 293

Editor's Note

Skip and Gabi's manuscript appealed to me as an editor because of my own gypsy spirit. When I was 23 years old, I bought a small sailing sloop for $3000, made her seaworthy, and set off on a series of adventures with $30 in my pocket. I learned the importance of self-sufficiency, came to value material things based on needs rather than wants, and learned how to live life efficiently and fully. I odd-jobbed my way through the Bahamas, played guitar for change in Gibraltar's pedestrian tunnels, and lived like a king on little more than air. Occasionally, I found "real opportunities" to work in small ad agencies or perform in nightclubs. I imagine my monthly budget averaged out to about $200/month, but I never missed a meal, never borrowed money, never begged for food, and always had a warm, safe, dry place to sleep. (I do remember getting sick of eating lobster every day once when I hit a financial dry spell.)

Despite the warnings of friends and family, I found jobs and opportunities and good people waiting when I got back. I didn't "lose my career skills" or "lose touch with what the job market requires." Clever people will always find a place to "plug in," and if your quality of life interests are sufficiently strong to have piqued your interest in Skip and Gabi's book, you're likely just such a clever person. And if you do go, you'll find it's actually *much* more difficult to survive in the land of clocks and calendars than it is on the road or out in the adjacent woods.

The biggest obstacle to living fully is fear—mostly fear of imaginary threats. I was afraid to sail my boat by myself every time I hauled the anchor. I was afraid to sail 38 days across the Atlantic. I was once afraid to offer my services as a professional editor because others had decades more experience than me. But I'm a better person for having accomplished these humble things.

An hour a day on the expressway makes for far more dangerous circumstances than a North Atlantic gale in mid-ocean—and it's a lot less inspiring. Avoidance of fear leads to a lot of lying around watching television, but it does little to reduce life's real dangers. What scares *me* most is the notion of getting old and reflecting on a life of things I wish I had done but never did.

Skip and Gabi offer useful formulas, inspiring people, sound ideas and winning perspectives. They did it; a lot of other people have done it; and you can do it. What *it* is is for you to define—it might involve a well-funded trip to Asia; it could mean a $30 sailing trip; or it may be as simple as a perspective adjustment that changes your relationship between working and living.

Just Go! is superficially a book about life on the road, but it's as much a book about life. Read, enjoy, and then go live yours to the fullest. You'll find plenty of inspiration in these pages.

—*Dave Bricker, Editor*

Preface

*T*he sun was still uncommitted as I strolled into my office, turned on the lights and launched into yet another Monday morning.

I sipped scalding coffee as I powered up my computer and scrolled through the first flurries of what would soon become the daily email blizzard. My eyes fell on one item—a draft of a press release announcing a corporate restructuring I had been working on for weeks. It quoted me as head of global sales and identified the three regional vice presidents who would report to me as the company reorganized and began another round of competitive strategies to grow and improve our business.

What would this change mean for me? There would be hand-shakes and backslapping, phone calls and emails of congratulations, a small congratulatory party, perhaps, replete with the predictable trappings of yet another upward career move.

It would mean more responsibility, more work.

I sat back at my desk and stared over Boston's City Hall Plaza, thinking. I picked up the phone and called my boss in New York, *wrapping up the conversation in about 10 minutes. Then I called my wife.*

"I just quit my job," I told her.

Introduction

*I**f you are one of the millions who are quietly discontent to endlessly run on the treadmill but are locked in place, this book is for you. This book is about making choices and embracing options that will liberate you to enjoy living. A life of exploration, learning and experience awaits.***

I used to obsess about money.

I used to worry a lot.

I used to dread Sundays.

Sundays had become loathsome beasts.

Like a nor'easter gathering off the coast of Massachusetts, a gnawing angst would descend upon me around mid-day as the weekend came to a close. It grew in strength as the day progressed. Around sundown, the notion that Sunday becomes Monday would ruin my mood, turning me sullen, downcast.

The pattern became worse in the aftermath of the great global economic downturn. But this was more than dissatisfaction, deeper than a sense of detachment from work, family life and purpose. There seemed no antidote, no solution to the core question I constantly asked myself: *Why am I not happy?*

On the surface, I had everything: a fantastic wife and a happy marriage, two wonderful daughters, good health and a great job that paid me well. We entertained often and traveled several times a year. My kids went to terrific universities and emerged with no personal debt.

Yet every Sunday I grappled with the unsettling feeling that I was living a life that didn't feel like it was mine. I felt trapped, stuck.

The feeling was different for Gabi. She'd grown up overseas and had lived around the world most of her life. She didn't have the ties and commitment to family and relationships that bound me to the U.S. Our partnership had been formed in our mid-lives, so we brought two unique and very different perspectives to the precipice of "what's next?"

Like countless others on the treadmill pursuing the American dream, I'd been lured into the traditional career path. In the late 70s I bypassed college graduation to head straight to work. I worked my way up the ladder through a career in media, peaking as a senior executive in a global news organization. The years unfolded as job and life changes carried me on like a river's current.

Week in and week out, my life remained fairly constant. I had bought into the notion that success and happiness meant a nose stuck to the grindstone, and a commitment to a future measured week-by-week, rooted in consumerism and fueled by competition.

On the surface, it looked like success, but Sundays had become a problem.

The mornings would begin just fine with a walk through our sleepy seaside community north of Boston to one of our haunts for a leisurely breakfast, followed by some exercise, time with family and friends—normal, "every weekend" stuff. But around 2 or 3 in the afternoon, the low-grade discontentment would begin, chewing at first in my stomach, then up through my chest and into my temples.

Monday loomed. Work—with its myriad pressures and demands—would begin anew, and the cycle of "show up, do the work and get paid" would repeat.

Depression would settle in as I contemplated a new start to yet another week—a feeling similar to being in a bad relationship that needed to end.

It wasn't just the job or the work, though. The problem felt a lot deeper, bigger.

As months passed, the feeling became more pervasive, more urgent. An expanding intellectual, moral and spiritual void lay at the core of the emptiness I felt. It seemed as though I was cheating more than myself by blithely continuing.

I began to ask myself big questions. *What am I looking for? What's missing? Will I allow complacency and inertia to block my quest for personal satisfaction?* I despised the idea of running away from my problems, as I am naturally wired to confront my demons and shout them into submission. I tried to "control" my problem through reason, regular exercise and therapy.

I ate too much, drank too much, bought too much.

The problem remained.

I made lists of goals and hopes. I wrote letters to myself. I quit my job a hundred times in my mind. But I always stopped short of taking action, mired in an endless loop of questions without answers. The dilemma felt huge, at times unsolvable. Work/life balance was an ephemeral notion, a distant goal.

Not only did I have concerns about finding something new and uplifting for my future, I also had concerns about others in my life. I'd become disinterested in my work and had developed a lack of focus and a lousy attitude. My co-workers suffered due to my lack of passion for my job. My family had to deal with my irritability showing up like clockwork on Sundays (and sometimes during the week).

I developed a keen awareness of people who were living life-styles I envied and admired. Like an ant drawn to a picnic, I found myself attracted to people whose lives gave them choice, options and exciting experiences.

One of them was a client. I don't recall her name, but her story remains clear. She was European and working as an investor relations professional in the late 1990s for a publicly traded technology company outside Boston. She had a compelling, light, free-spiritedness that was uncommon among her peers in the world of finance.

As I came to know her better, she let me in on her personal story: she was working to make some money while she and her husband took time off from their round-the-world bicycle trip. She wouldn't be around for much longer—the call of the road beckoned.

Her story intrigued me, and it subconsciously ate away at my comfort zone. It reminded me there was a world of experience and wonder out there that I would never see without making a change. I became more interested and began to consider my options.

Every Monday morning, when I padded into my kitchen and started a pot of coffee, I would turn on my Blackberry and listened disconsolately as the incoming messages piled up. As the months passed, I gradually turned my daily despair into action. I looked for a way out of my professional and social maze. Mornings became less about checking the daily news and all about looking for a new path to chart. I started to research— new jobs, different places to live, new lifestyles. As I probed into the worlds that unfolded on my PC, my objective became clearer. We needed a change—a big one.

Gabi was running a small startup business from our home, so she was unencumbered by traditional work obligations and ready to hit the road well before I got ready to pack.

As we opened the door to what might be next we discovered many people who shared our dissatisfaction with status quo, our unease with convention and our wishes for something better. Their stories inspired us, warmed our hearts and informed us. Each offered lessons with messages worth paying attention to.

Mike, a former corporate exec and his wife Terri, had bolted from the buttoned-down life to volunteer with a Caribbean-based organization while living in Florida with their children. It was much less lucrative but far more rewarding work, and it filled a widening spiritual void for Mike.

John and Karlene had been serial budget world travelers for many years and were looking for their next adventure. They lived out of a suitcase for months at a time, only returning home briefly to visit their families and stock up for their next travel experience.

We met these people through happenstance and through mutual acquaintances—or through acts of divine intervention. They inspired us, and set the tone for a process that led us to live outside of the U.S. Their stories—and those of many others we met along the way—opened our minds.

Our collective experiences with the process of leaving life in corporate, commoditized America, form the backbone of *Just Go!*

This book chronicles our journey from a life of comfortable existence to one of exploration and adventure. It's an account of how we decided to take a chance that the rewards of dramatic change would far outweigh the challenges. In writing this, we wanted to reveal the angst, the thought, the planning and, ultimately, the acceptance of risk as we set out to permanently change our lives.

We also included stories of people from all walks of life: married with children, single, in committed relationships, straight, gay, well off and nearly broke. They all have one thing in common: a commitment to embrace change not as a threat but as life's greatest opportunity, and dedication to a lifestyle far more rewarding than what they had left behind.

It took a while for us to ease into this mode, but looking back now our sole regret is that we didn't get at it sooner.

My Uncle Wes, as insightful and honest a man as I've met, looked me in the eye not long after we began our process of "dismounting." "You've changed," he told me during a round of golf. "You're not the angry young man you were. It's all gone."

Many others who know me best say they can see it, too, and I find those reactions validating and reassuring. It's great to know that the positive effects of living a life of choice and personal freedom not only feed my physical and spiritual self, but that it's obvious to others, too.

This book is about the process we went through to give ourselves a break and get on with our lives. It's about our metamorphosis and the gifts it has provided. We weighed our options and charted a course based on the process, facts and figures that led us to the brink of opportunity.

We ended our survey of the people we interviewed with one final query: What is your core message to our readers?

Their collective response: *Don't wait. Do it now.* You will be glad you did. Mostly, though, they advised that you work tirelessly to identify, pursue and fulfill your dreams—whatever they may be.

Since taking the plunge, we've learned that quitting the rat race is a hell of a lot easier and infinitely more rewarding than we had imagined. The pitfalls have been few and often rewarding, instructive and at times hilarious. The experiences have filled our lives, minds and hearts and made us feel much closer to the world around us.

Gabi and I have each other to lean on and shape our dreams as we proceed during our journey, but many we spoke with have tackled much higher mountains on their own—and have prospered along the way.

I no longer obsess about money.

I don't worry as much.

I no longer dread Sundays.

> Skip and Gabi Yetter
> Phnom Penh, Cambodia, 2010–2013
> On the move since then with no end in sight.
> www.TheMeanderthals.com

TALES FROM THE ROAD
ACTION PLAN

MAYBE YOU'RE LIKE ME - DISSATISFIED WITH MY LIFE AND INTRIGUED BY THE PROSPECT OF CREATING A NEW LIFE. MAYBE I'LL LIVE IN ANOTHER CULTURE, I THOUGHT, OR SIMPLY MAKE A BREAK FROM A JOB THAT DIDN'T WORK FOR ME ANY LONGER.

I WOULD LIE AWAKE AT NIGHT, THINKING ABOUT WHAT WOULD MAKE ME HAPPY, OR WHERE I'D LIKE TO BE. I DREAMED ABOUT IT, SO I BEGAN TO WRITE MY THOUGHTS DOWN FOR FUTURE REFERENCE. WRITING DOWN YOUR THOUGHTS GIVES LICENSE TO DREAM. A PLAN MAKES DREAMS REALITY.

HOW TO BEGIN?

WRITE A LETTER TO YOURSELF OUTLINING WHAT YOUR BIG-PICTURE GOALS AND ASPIRATIONS FOR THE NEXT YEAR OR THREE.

MAKE A LIST OF WHAT'S IMPORTANT: MONEY, FREEDOM, NEW EXPERIENCES, BIG CHANGE, OR A MODEST TWEAK ON A LIFE THAT'S IN NEED OF A NEW BATTERY.

REVISIT YOUR LIST, ADD AND REMOVE ITEMS, AND KEEP IT AROUND AND VISIBLE SO IT'S PART OF YOUR LIFE. GIVE YOURSELF SOME SORT OF DEADLINE TO COMPLETE THE LIST, CONDUCT PRIMARY RESEARCH, OR MAKE A DECISION ON MAKING YOUR MOVE.

TOO OFTEN WE DREAM, ENVISION AND ANALYZE, BUT FAIL TO ACT.

I
Identifying the Disease

*D*usk *lingered as I pulled into the driveway at our harborside home. The light shone brightly from the living room, inviting me into an atmosphere of welcoming calm after yet another tumultuous day doing work that had long since lost meaning.*

"How was your day?" Gabi greeted me with a kiss. My sullen look provided an answer before I spoke.

"More of the same," I responded glumly. "Wins and losses, comings and goings, stuff with the boss. Not sure how much more of this I can take, really." I dropped my briefcase in my home office, parked my Blackberry in the cradle next to my PC so it would recharge and download any current messages to my remote VPN link, and leave me alone for a while.

Abandoning the world of corporate management, I headed to the living room, a glass of red wine in hand, and sank into the sofa next to Gabi.

"So what are we going to do with you?" she asked, provoking the latest iteration of a conversation we'd had dozens of times. I thought of the books I'd read about career changes, about being happy, about conversations I'd had with people I respected about making a change in my life. I recalled the countless paths I had explored that had turned to dead ends, leaving me treading water in a financially rewarding but spiritually draining job.

"If I have to endure one more Go2Meeting, one more PowerPoint presentation, one more financial review of an underperforming office, I think I'm going to snap," I whined.

Gabi has always had a way of providing me with both the support and the boot in the rear I so dearly need. "Maybe it's just time," she said, in her lilting British accent. "You know what you have to do."

Our interest in making a radical change to our lives turned into a burning desire after I read a book by an English business-man who had shed his skin as a corporate executive, joined the Buddhist order in England, got rid of everything and bolted for a life as a monk in Thailand. While shaving my head and donning a saffron robe is about as likely as me becoming a Yankees fan, I was inspired by Peter Robinson's story. *Phra Farang* (roughly translated, Foreign Monk) turned out to be a pivotal catalyst for my change of thinking.

I'd heard of Robinson while travelling in Thailand in 2007 and was struck by his story. He, too, had been overwhelmed by the void that went along with a life of material things, career and money. It was as though he'd been infected with a spiritual parasite; his contentment declined as his wealth and collection of material goods increased.

He sounded a lot like me.

I'd looked into buying *Phra Farang* online but hadn't gotten around to making the purchase. How I finally bought and read it was yet another eerie experience of divine coincidence—an alignment of the stars in my favor.

While visiting friends and family a year or so after our honeymoon in Thailand, Gabi and I stopped into a bookstore in London. Waiting for her on the bookstore floor while she visited the loo, I was drawn to the title on the spine of a book among hundreds in a shelf 50 or so feet across the room.

Phra Farang.

I recognized the word "farang" (foreigner) and remembered my conversation with an expat in Chiang Mai about Robinson, his chosen path, and his book. Excited and with a sense that something significant had just happened, I bought the book

and devoured it over the next few days. I will forever be mysti-
fied by what led me to it—displayed among hundreds of others,
competing for attention with colors, words and designs—and
extremely grateful to whatever forces brought us together that
fateful day.

One moment, one phrase, one book. The process had begun.

Robinson had been king of the consumer mountain, living
an entitled life of homes, cars, travel, food, fine wine, friends
and money-fueled choices. But the spiritual void within him
began to expand when he visited a Buddhist temple outside of
London and he became intrigued by Buddhism. *Phra Farang*
details his experiences as he shed his corporate skin, rid himself
of his possessions and ultimately moved to Thailand where he
became the tallest and whitest monk in a temple in Chiang Mai.

Robinson's message was like a Hilton Sunday brunch banquet
for a starving man. I wanted Robinson's life, not as a monk but
as a man freed from the yoke of obligation. He wrote of the
purifying feeling of getting rid of possessions, and how it felt to
direct energy previously spent in pursuit of money into a spiritual quest.

The book gave me the idea, power and authority to think
differently, to dream. *Phra Farang*—as well as Lee Eisenberg's
The Number, William Least Heat Moon's *Blue Highways,*
John Steinbeck's *Travels with Charley* and Jack Kerouac's *On the
Road* were important books that changed the way I approached

my life. I'd read Steinbeck's and Kerouac's tomes earlier, but I wasn't was as ready to fully appreciate their message then as I was when I hit my 50s.

These books have several common themes that appealed to me: roguish individualism, exploration, the expansion of one's individual universe. But mostly, it seems to me, they're about change. Some people hate change. Some, like Gabi, love it, embracing new challenges and opportunities like a child tucking into an ice cream sundae. And some—like moi—engage in a lengthy dance with change that falls somewhere between avoidance/acceptance and manic pursuit of something new.

"Get busy living or get busy dying," narrates Morgan Freeman in a key line from one of my favorite movies, The Shawshank Redemption. Prescient, inspirational words, those. And they've become something of a personal mantra as I've discovered a new way of life.

My shift in attitude came from necessity.

Well into midlife, I was stuck. I was locked in place by a system that seemed designed to keep me right where I was: earning great money and creating a terrific sub-economy by buying, going, doing and giving. Some might argue that consuming at that level was no better or worse than any other form of self-medication. I'd have a hard time disagreeing.

Tracking the latest job dissatisfaction statistics and driven by the spiritual void that went along with an increasingly meaningless work/life combination, I found myself struggling more and more with the senseless pursuit of money, doing work that meant less and less to me as the years spun by.

Something was missing. A powerful and significant part of me was dormant; I was a somnambulist doing an eight-hour sleepwalk every day, growing increasingly resentful of a work/life paradigm that held me in place.

Once the questions began and the research followed, an avalanche of emotion and sentiments made the status quo an unacceptable option. This was anything but a simple problem.

It took me three years to focus on the core questions and find the answers.

It took me less than two hours to make the decision to quit my job on that fateful and wonderful Monday morning.

But what about the steps in between? What of the sleepless nights, long evenings sitting side by side with my wife on our comfortable sofa, talking? Thinking? Dreaming?

I didn't like where I stood.

At 54 years of age, I figured I'd have had to work another 15 years while saving half of my annual income (fat chance) to meet the recommended investment goal. I'd bought into the paradigm that most investment counselors preach: You'll need enough capital to generate 70% to 80% of your current income to maintain an inflation-adjusted standard of living.

According to an online work life expectancy calculator, here's how the rest of my life would have shaped up had we remained in the U.S.: I could have expected to retire at 67, and then live 13 additional years until my personal clock is projected to run out. (As MarketWatch's Bob Powell likes to point out, people in their late 50s have roughly 10,000 days to live.) I am out to prove them all wrong, and genetics seems on my side. My mom lived to the age of 89; dad passed away at 82. I intend to hang around longer than either of them. In fact, one of those nifty Facebook games we all play recently revealed that I am going to live to the ripe old age of 104.

This would have meant another decade plus behind the desk, and then a brief respite before my time was theoretically up. That was a humbling scenario to contemplate. It didn't offer enough time, enough freedom, enough choice.

I found the reality of my work life expectancy depressing, and more than a little bit irritating. I felt as though I'd been lied to—by the financial services industry, by my government and by the genius expert buzzmongers who perpetuated fear, kept me locked in commuter hell and who made a ton of money while doing exactly nothing to actually help. Now, years removed from the corporate life and firmly ensconced in a life of choice, the notion of stagnancy seems vaguely unpleasant, like a faint memory of a wisdom tooth extraction.

As one of 146 million workers in the U.S., I had been conditioned to accept the realities that go with the life of a career guy. I'd had my share of success and owned a beautiful home near the ocean in an upscale Boston suburb. I had lots of stuff and was in the enviable position of being able to make loads of decisions about how to spend my downtime and my money. Yet I was increasingly frustrated with the status quo. Turns out I had a lot of company, and the numbers are growing.

A 2012 Right Management employee satisfaction survey revealed that 65% of respondents want to quit their jobs. Sure, many of these people fall into the "grass is greener" camp, longing for a job with better pay, shorter hours, fewer headaches, more or less (pick one) responsibility, authority, independence, etc. But many of these unhappy clock-watchers just want out.

This "unhappy laborer" statistic is all the more stunning when you consider that millions of workers are delaying retirement by as much as five years due to the chunk taken out of their retirement savings by the economic collapse of 2008. The U.S. economy has recovered, but most research demonstrates that baby boomers aren't getting back the lost years during which their savings ought to have been compounding interest.

And this has affected retirees' attitudes.

According to a September 2014 report by the Pension Research Council of the Wharton School of the University of Pennsylvania, workers' confidence in having enough money for a comfortable retirement took a sharp hit in 2007 and has yet to rebound. From 1990 to 2007, the study says, confidence in a comfortable retirement hovered over 70%. It dropped to 47% during the economic crisis before rebounding to 57% in 2014.

Some of this lack of confidence may be attributed to the soft job market for retirees; the report claims: there are simply fewer jobs to provide supplemental income for people who have moved on from their careers.

Increased resentment at work combined with anticipation of more years of the same sounds like trouble brewing. Thinking about retirement? Using what resources, and supporting what kind of lifestyle, and where?

The facts reveal a depressing reality: most people face a life in retirement that is hardly what they envisioned. The widely marketed images of gray-haired people with perfectly white teeth laughing away the days on the golf courses, in restaurants and with family seem horribly overstated. These days, such images seem more appropriate for Cialis ads than for the promise of a realistic, happy and secure retirement.

Exempt from this unhappy profile, of course, are the legions of one-percenters—the fortunate and exclusive portion of the population that has managed to cobble together the majority of wealth in the United States.

Since 2011, more than 10,000 people in the U.S. alone have turned 65 every day, and according to the Pew Research Center, that number will continue until 2029. That's a lot of people soon to be looking for answers to tough questions like: What now?

While generally agreeing that the financial situation facing most retirees isn't ideal, even the experts can't agree on what constitutes a financially viable retirement for U.S. workers. They also disagree widely on how much money people have in the bank and what the fallout will be when millions of people suddenly confronted with retirement see a future that is considerably less fulfilling and secure than they had expected.

A 2014 Employee Benefit Research Institute (ERBI) survey revealed that 60% of U.S. workers at all stages of their careers reported having less than $25,000 in savings set aside for retirement; 36% of these workers say they have less than $1,000 in savings. This number was up from 20% in 2009 and 28% in 2013.

Experts' estimates of retirees' projected savings varies widely. The highest average I found in my research was $187,000; the lowest was $29,000. None of these estimates paint a rosy picture for retirees planning to rely on savings to supplement Social Security, no matter where in the U.S. they may choose to live.

What about the safety net Uncle Sam has supposedly been holding for us all these years?

The average monthly U.S. Social Security benefit for a 66-year-old retiree is $1,294 or $2,111 if you're a couple receiving benefits (2014). Absent a fairly serious adjustment in lifestyle, most people will have a tough time living on Social Security alone. So what does the average Joe need to enjoy a fruitful and happy retirement?

"You'd need $1 million in nest egg to generate $40,000 in income on top of Social Security," said Powell, retirement editor at MarketWatch. That's a reference to the tiny chunk of the population fortunate enough to plan retiring off investment returns. It's not representative of most American retirees.

This partially explains why more and more retirement-age individuals have been delaying retirement. Many had planned to work part-time after they quit the rat race even before the bottom fell out of the markets and sliced a third out of most people's 401(k) accounts. Now, the predicament is worse.

One factor is the cost of living in the United States. Average household expenses in the U.S. were $51,000 in 2013, according to a Bureau of Labor Statistics report (Sept. 9, 2014), including housing, food, healthcare, entertainment and transportation.

It doesn't take advanced mathematics skills to see that these numbers don't add up to a relaxed, confident and comfortable retirement.

So what do to?

Plenty of retirement guides help you figure out how to live on what you have, and all sorts of websites, blogs and books describe the relative costs of living in Costa Rica, Panama, Thailand or even Croatia, so I'm not going into that here. For us, the question was never about living cheaply, but about living well.

As I researched our options and did the personal work to be clear about what I really wanted, it became obvious that our path was going to take us some somewhere different. I mean someplace *really* different—in all respects—a place that would offer the right mix of freedom, the opportunity to learn (a new culture, language, history), and personal challenges, while also giving us a chance to give something back to others.

Our choices for change included a new relationship with money that started with a serious examination of our roles as consumers. As we rid our lives of accumulated things, we began to realize how much happiness we found in living simply. We stopped buying on impulse, then stopped buying everything but essentials.

At some point in this process it occurred to me: The U.S. consumer society teaches us that we're supposed to use money to buy into a way of life, but maybe that's backwards. Maybe your money—no matter how much or little you have—will be better utilized to buy out of a way of life, and into something simpler, gentler, better.

That became a driving force in our lives.

Buried in the avalanche of online information are tons of people searching for answers. And if their thinking is anything like what was going on between my ears, the traditional thought process has been far too narrow, the considered options far too few.

The financial services industry, in its self-interested pursuit to do what's best for you while making billions in profits along the way, is pushing you to save, invest, plan and worry that whatever you do simply isn't going to be enough—not by a long shot. Like Bluto Blutarsky in Animal House, the personal finance wizards are screaming "Who's with me?" as they run out the door and down the street, satchels full of your money in hand, with a paltry fortunate few on their heels.

What about the rest of us?

Nearly a decade passed before U.S. workers regained the same per capita income they had enjoyed prior to the Great Depression of 1929. The recent recovery took a faster course, but it has still set pre-retirees back several years. But current worries—fanned by online opinions like a Southern California wildfire—are rooted in more than how much you earn or have in the bank. There's the unhappy trend of uncontrollable costs.

Take healthcare, for example. A 2013 survey by Deloitte Center for Financial Services found that 60% of pre-retirees believe that healthcare costs will consume their savings *regardless* of how much they're able to save.

An April 2014 MarketWatch article reported that a couple retiring in 2015 with average benefits will likely spend 70% of their Social Security on medical costs during their retirement. Quoting research from HealthView Services, Inc., MarketWatch said the average Social Security income of $2,111 per month would be consumed by the $366,000 of combined costs of Medicare Parts B and D, plus supplemental insurance during the course of their retirement. Fidelity Investments and EBRI estimate a slight less bleak picture: both estimate post-retirement medical costs at around $220,000, MarketWatch's Powell says.

Whatever you think of the Affordable Care Act, most seem to agree that creating a framework for fair and equitable health-care for all U.S. citizens will at least start to arrest what otherwise had been an uncontrolled financial train wreck for all of us.

I'm no longer part of the work force and even I get stressed by all this stuff.

So what to do about all of this? Work until you die? Suck it up and get ready for a dramatically reduced lifestyle as you confront retirement? As the era of company-sponsored pensions comes to a conclusive and unhappy close, is it the fate of retirees to adopt a lesser standard of living in order to remain in their homes, stay close to their families and continue to access friends and doctors?

It simply made no sense to us to continue laboring onward toward an unacceptable and unattainable goal that failed to give us choices and the personal and spiritual growth we desired. It made no sense to me to quit, dial back our lifestyle to a bare-bones existence (though this offers a perfectly acceptable and attractive proposition in its own right), but otherwise remain in the same place.

The numbers didn't add up, even though by most standards we'd had good fortune and a decent nest egg upon which to build our future. If we were to remain in the U.S., living the same standard of living, it meant I was far from done running on the treadmill.

As I began to question the foundation for my future, I started broadening my thinking. I read everything I could get my hands on, first by researching online, but I got serious when I read a book my friend Steve Gregory gave to me. In his informative, influential and easy to read book *The Number,* Lee Eisenberg examines not the oft-marketed question of how to provide for oneself in retirement but how to create a healthy balance between financial security and your chosen lifestyle. It's about achieving balance. Eisenberg outlines some important variables: how you live, what choices you make concerning the circumstances under which you spend your time and where you live, among others.

Whoa, wait! Where you live? As in, *live somewhere else?* Like one of the amazing places in the U.S. and abroad that my wife and I had visited over the years? I'd never really considered living outside the U.S., but as I read *The Number* it became clear to me that limiting our lives to U.S. soil carried a pretty steep price.

Eisenberg introduced the rest of the equation to me and got me thinking that by adjusting our lifestyle (where and how we live, what we own, and what relationship we have with consuming) we could be in a position to step off the treadmill.

Not at some point in the future. Right NOW!

Throwing convention to the hounds, I met with our financial planner and told him my goals: I wanted to stop working full time and I wanted to know how much we could realistically expect to draw each year while protecting our principal. I held my breath as the verdict came in. Once we knew the figures, we got to work filling in the details of constructing a new life.

We made the commitment to dramatically cut our costs, starting with the mortgage (sell the house) and car expenses (live without them). We would work to supplement our income, part-time, on a consulting basis, or as freelance writers.

And we would do it living somewhere other than in the U.S.

A core of savings made it feasible. A simple math exercise validated the concept. Our honeymoon had given me an idea. The rest of the facts sent me searching for airline tickets and researching costs of living in Southeast Asia.

Eisenberg's book helped change my life and dramatically influenced our decision to bag it all, pack it in and bolt for a country

that offered far more for a helluva lot less. His core message
to me: Our lives are about creating and honoring a real and
honest respect for what's important, and an open commitment
to embracing something different. It meant that Gabi and I
would be required to honestly assess the cornerstones of our
life foundation, testing each underpinning for its true value.
Finishing the book, I realized my duty to get on with it.

So I did. And that meant envisioning a different lifestyle in
a different place, probably far away from those I love and the
places that had been a part of my life for over half a century.

More than that, I wanted to do something to give back.
The voices of giving and volunteering were shouting down the
screams promoting responsibility and duty.

And so began our journey to Cambodia. Compared to the
predictable alternative of dutifully trudging along in the U.S.
workplace, I like where I'm sitting. It turns out we're far from
alone, in terms of people who have chosen to live somewhere
other than the country of their birth.

As of early 2013, of the 314 million people in the U.S., 143
million constituted the workforce. A whopping 12 million of
them were unemployed. Another 68 million Americans were
receiving retirement or other SSI (disability) benefits. More than
500,000 retirees receive their checks as they spend their days in
countries other than the U.S.

But not everyone wants to hustle off to Chiang Mai, set up shop in Domenical or learn the samba in Buenos Aires without a plan or at least some foresight. Thinking big about your future means starting with small steps.

As we made major changes in our lives, we discovered many others who'd done the same, some with as little as $900 in the bank and some with two or three kids in tow. All of them have something in common: They had the discipline, courage and motivation to envision a positive change and put their wishes into action.

But what about the 130 or so million people who are still slogging away? It seems as though people are fatter, unhappier, saving less and working harder and longer than ever. And with little hope on the horizon from the intelligentsia in Washington and Wall Street, we are all on our own now more than ever.

For us—and for the families and individuals we interviewed for this book—the idea of staying put was unacceptable. Life as we knew it presented us with distasteful options and lacked the richness, diversity and personal challenges we felt were important for scratching our intellectual and spiritual itches. The idea of staying on the treadmill failed to satisfy the half-million or so retirees who have fled to other shores to spend their post-work years in lands where the dollar buys more and life is much less complicated.

We looked at the future and didn't like what we saw.

We decided to get out.

Like the others we interviewed for this book (Section Two — Stories from the Other Side of Convention—details their experiences), our new life began with the decision to make a change.

In 2010 Gabi and I moved from Massachusetts to Cambodia, taking a plunge we had imagined for years but for many reasons hadn't implemented. A change like that seemed abstract and unthinkable. Family commitments and concerns, money, career, worries about long-term financial and personal security—all the aspects of life that are woven into the workaday existence in the United States of America—all pressed ominously upon me like a cloud blocking the sun over the freshly-planted field of personal opportunity and growth.

Since leaving the U.S., our lives have been rich with fascinating experiences involving new cultures, food, languages and challenges. We are different people now, with new preferences and priorities. We've had an attitude overhaul fed by a new set of values.

For the first time our lives lack a "big picture" plan. A Type-A business guy by nature, I had always had a clear sense of career path, personal and professional growth, but as time passed that balance began to tip in the wrong direction.

Work dominated my life. The older I grew the more unsettled I became. "Work is only one of the things I do," I loved to say, quoting my friend Fred Oakes, but I let my pursuit of career and money dominate and define me. And that led to the misery that descended upon me every Sunday afternoon.

Work began to take more from me than it gave, but quitting meant committing to a major life change. On paper, it was a horrible time to jump blindly into the ranks of the unemployed, if one paid close attention to the statistics and bought into the traditional plan of working toward retirement. I was at the peak of my earning power in a secure position while the market was shedding jobs at an alarming rate. Out of work middle-aged employees were having a tough time re-entering the workforce. Job security meant everything.

This was the first exposure I would have to an interesting phenomenon of perceived self-worth, a pattern that revealed itself over the next few months. In the business world you're either in or out, and the power structure seems protective of itself. Once I declared my intentions, I gave up my ad hoc membership in "the club" of corporate identity. "Former SVP of Global Sales" says "retired" to many, and it lacks the currency of one who is still firmly in the saddle.

I sensed a shift in attitude from colleagues and work friends. Titles and authority bring power, and one of the byproducts is respect or capitulation to higher authority. I suddenly knew what it must feel like to be a lame-duck politician—stripped of authority and voice, no longer a player in the game of opportunity or a foe to be reckoned with. I found myself neutered in the business world, a bench player instead a member of the starting team.

I reevaluated countless relationships—both in business and in my personal life.

Depressed, I spent a month sleeping a lot, walking the streets of Marblehead and tucked away in deep thought in our rental condo.

Everything had changed.

"Friendships" that had previously flourished suddenly disappeared. Invitations to fundraisers, parties and golf outings declined, and my network shrunk. At first it depressed and worried me, but after several weeks I came to reevaluate and appreciate the relationships that remained. I shifted my focus to the ones that mattered, as I had in my post-divorce years.

I learned skills in those first few months that have served me ever since.

As we developed our new lifestyle, we learned the fun and wonder of winging it, trusting and going with the flow, and anticipating challenges in foreign lands as fantastic opportunities to learn new skills and explore the limits of our expectations about life.

In the next few years we often got lost, and in the process learned that losing our way often leads to the best experiences of all.

We are far from being alone with this mindset. Each of the people included in this book (Section Two—Stories from the Other Side of Convention—begins on page 171), made a conscious decision to dramatically change their lives. And each chose to live somewhere other than the country of his or her birth. Read through the threads of wisdom in their voices of experience; their messages may be applied to any significant life change you might be considering.

Like most of our interview subjects, ours was not an impulsive decision but one based on a careful examination of what matters most to us. That took a lot of soul searching, along with considerable personal discipline to stop fooling ourselves. It was disproportionately *my* issue, too, since I was the one with five decades of history and tradition as an American citizen with deep family ties to Massachusetts. To get where I wanted to be, I had to be real and honest with myself.

I entered the tunnel on this road of robust change an unfulfilled man, not entirely miserable but not happy. I emerged a different man with a different outlook, a new agenda and an openness I had never felt I had within me.

II
Researching and Soul Searching

A trickle of sweat ran down the back of my neck. I pushed open the heavy wooden door to our room in the Baan Orapin guesthouse and kicked off my flipflops. A sliver of moon shone through the carved shutters, casting a shadow across the silk bedspread as I poured two glasses of chilled wine and switched on the ceiling fan. "How about renting a motorbike tomorrow and visiting the Doi Sutep temple?" Gabi's voice called out from the balcony. I was silent. My mind swirled with possibility and excitement. I thought about our past week in Thailand—about the gentle, spiritual people, about how it felt to walk along the potholed road past ramshackle houses, undeveloped tracts of land strewn with trash and garbage, and among countless unfamiliar faces beaming with smiles. I thought about the stories I'd heard from other people who'd moved here on a shoestring budget to discover their own personal Nirvana.

My next words changed our lives forever: "Gabi, how would you feel about living here?"

Deciding to leave the U.S. was like ending a bad relationship. My life at work conflicted with what I wanted to do, though

I truly had no idea what that specifically might be. I felt locked in place, surrounded to a point of surrender by a regimen that had become increasingly foreign. I wanted out, but I felt change was impossible without unacceptable sacrifices and conditions.

Repetition ruled my days.

I have always been a man of extremes. At once tolerant while hopelessly hyper-impatient, throughout the years I would plod along in unhappy work or personal circumstances until something within me snapped and forced me to make a change. Along the way I'd make lists, examine the problem from all angles, and agonize over details.

Quitting life in America and departing U.S. shores was no different. It took years of analysis and anguish, conversations and consideration of all the options. Once the decision was made, though, it was only a matter of distancing ourselves from the physical stuff that bound us.

After several months and no offers we finally attracted a buyer and sold our house. Taking a loss as the U.S. housing market plummeted in the wake of the recession, we moved into a rental condo. I viewed the loss on the home sale as a cost of not doing business that we had calculated and accepted; it was anticipated pain that we figured into our financial equation.

Selling the house proved to be a cathartic and emancipating exercise that demonstrated how little Gabi and I truly cared about much of the stuff we had acquired over the years.

The kayaks went to friends who had always wanted a pair. The snow blower and deck furniture were shipped off to my niece and her husband. Much of our home's furniture went to another niece and a nephew, both of whom had recently bought their first homes and were happy to have stuff with which to fill their empty rooms.

The few heirlooms and boxes of keepsakes we couldn't part with went into a storage bin near our former home. Now, we visit once a year to update seasonal clothes, reminisce and stare in a baffled state of amusement at the stacks of stuff we will probably never use again. Neither of us is certain what's in all those boxes. I giggle, thinking that it may fall to my daughters at some point to pore over my 1973 Greenfield High School yearbook, and ponder aloud what I was doing, perched in a tree with shoulder-length hair and a cigarette in hand in my junior college graduation photo.

Getting rid of our stuff proved to be spiritually rewarding. As our physical universe of things decreased, our inner peace grew and the world around us expanded. With less stuff, we felt poised to gain more from abstract, undefined, new sources. We began to consider possibilities that had previously been but whimsical notions.

I felt lighter, more fluid, more mobile. A minimalist life-style might be perfect for us, I thought, encouraged. I felt open, empowered, eager to probe new ideas, lifestyles, places to live. The winds of change were at my back.

As we settled into our rental condo, I worked in earnest to extricate myself from the working world and decide where to go. Simple living became an increasingly attractive compulsion. I love to cook and, having turned out many a fine meal on my professional gas stove and convection oven in our home, I worried how I would produce the same on a tiny stove that couldn't generate 35,000 BTU to properly sear salmon. (Three years later, I prepared pan-seared salmon with balsamic reduction on our apartment's four-burner cook stove in Phnom Penh. It was more a matter of finding salmon worth searing in Southeast Asian markets than figuring out a way to prepare it correctly. It turned out that finding good salmon in Phnom Penh was almost as easy as finding eager guests to help us eat it.)

A one-year lease in Marblehead gave us time to research, plan and plot our next move. Late summer turned to fall.

We knew Southeast Asia was our preferred destination. We had our sights set on Thailand but were open to other possibilities; we cast a wide net.

I didn't want to just quit and gather dust, as the idea of going from a fast-paced corporate environment to a life of golf, napping and lunch dates with friends sounded boring—a great way to slowly go nuts. I love cribbage but was not about to start hitting the Community Center on Tuesday afternoons. I'm far more inclined to head out for a solo mountain bike ride than I am to rally the mall walkers for a few pre-opening hour laps.

I come from stock that is wired to give back. My dad, who managed to find time in his life as a small business owner to serve several terms as an elected official in my hometown, was a big believer in helping out. After he sold his business and retired, he signed on to the federal Service Corps of Retired Executives (SCORE), offering his considerable business savvy and advice for free to small business owners. It was just one of the quiet contributions he made that left an indelible impression on me over the years.

Once, while hanging out together in our family's tiny cabin in the hills of western Massachusetts, I engaged him in a rare exchange about our life's courses.

"If you could re-make your life any way you could, what would you do?" I asked him.

He didn't hesitate. "I would jump in the car and drive around the country, stopping and talking to people and helping out where I could."

My dad had a profound impact on the way I conducted myself in life and in business and, while I saw the world in a broader context, my feelings about giving back paralleled his. Gabi and I looked at volunteer opportunities to build a bridge to where we wanted to go.

But it was my mom's big-heartedness and earnest spirit of giving that set the tone for my evolving spirit and gave me permission to embrace my new big ideas. A career giver, she was always the first to step up when someone was in need, quick with a batch of cookies and the first to reach for her checkbook when it came time to support the community hospital fund.

I got my first taste of international volunteerism when my friend and former boss Selma Williams invited me to join her in Ukraine to help post-Soviet era journalists convert their newspapers to private businesses with independent voices. The program—offered under the aegis of the International Research and Exchanges (IREX)—gave me a glimpse into the life of living and working in a place far from home.

The decision to dismount from corporate life in the U.S. arrived in a perfect storm of disparate events: chance meetings with like-minded people, writing the last of eight years' worth of college tuition checks for my daughters and the death of my mom at 89 at the hands of a fast-moving blood cancer.

It was an odd time, a mix of euphoric discoveries, long-sought answers to complicated questions and deeply saddening personal loss. Were my mother still alive—and I'd trade all the wonderful experiences we have had since leaving the U.S. for a few more years with her—there is no question that we would still be Stateside.

But her passing in 2009—much like the sale of our house and the final college tuition payment—seemed all part of a larger plan to free me from the ties that bound me to the U.S., and to a work situation that had failed to inspire me. She and I spoke about my interest in "going and doing," as she liked to say, and I know she heard the joy in my voice when I called her on her birthday from Mae Hong Son, Thailand. She understood my wish to live in Asia, though she had a hard time understanding what I would find so appealing about "living in Taiwan."

I learned well from her, though. An open heart and mind leaves one open to a world of boundless opportunities. Once I began to think differently, my universe of human contact began to shift. I began to encounter like-minded men who had become increasingly uncomfortable with the life of a corporate executive.

I discovered fascinating and inspirational role models. My new friends' experience, advice and counsel proved pivotal in my mindset change—as though a dormant part of my brain had kicked into overdrive. What was once a passing fantasy became a daily part of my life. The idea of living somewhere else fascinated, stimulated and drew me.

In an opinion column he penned for the New York Times in 2013, Graham Hill, founder of LifeEdited.com and TreeHugger. com explained his journey from being a wealthy beneficiary to building an Internet startup company in Seattle to becoming a minimalist world traveler with a new, more balanced view of the world. Not yet 30, Hill cashed in on the sale of his Internet consulting company in the late 90s and did what most people would do: he bought an enormous house and filled it with all kinds of cool stuff. Then he met a Spanish woman, fell in love and followed her to Spain, where they lived in a tiny flat with few possessions. Here, he had an epiphany: without ties that bound them, they were free to travel the world. They did, living in Buenos Aires, Bangkok and Toronto, creating some "do-gooder" companies along the way and embracing a lifestyle short on possessions but long on experiences and personal development.

Hill's story aligned with mine in many ways and was rooted in a couple of key guiding principles that resonate with me: Ask and the universe shall deliver. Imagine; then do.

Our dreams were fed by a new collection of like-minded friends, people who were either contemplating big changes or were already living on the other side of opting out. Our newfound friends encouraged us to talk substantively about leaving the U.S. and to spend time really thinking about where we might go and how we would live.

Books like *Phra Farang, On the Road* and *Travels with Charley* opened my eyes, but I needed more information about my options. That meant countless hours online, researching volunteer organizations and opportunities throughout SE Asia, and reading stories about people who had done what I had begun to imagine. Gabi and I formed a partnership of information gathering, exchanging links to articles that struck our fancy. We made a list of preferences so we could focus on the kinds of volunteer groups we were seeking: non-governmental, non-sectarian, flexible, small, (and preferably not teaching English, which is what many expat volunteers end up doing—not our cup of jasmine tea.)

"How about this?" "Check this out" or "Oh, my" became coded email subjects that flew back and forth as we divided our working hours between what we were paid to do and what truly interested us.

Leaving the U.S. became our number one topic of discussion; the subject was likely to come up during a drive or a quiet moment at home. It was exciting, new, different, and a bit scary. We came up with a list of features and benefits we wanted from volunteer organizations: health insurance, an on-the-ground support network wherever we landed, language instruction and the option for a longer-term contract in case we wanted to remain wherever we wound up. We wanted to be able to get to know the organization and its key players, and for them to know us. We didn't want to simply disappear; we could have done that on our own.

We considered the Peace Corps and went to an introductory session in Boston to kick the tires. My oldest daughter, my sister and my niece all had Peace Corps experience. We knew what a great organization it is and we were intrigued by the possibility, but the size, bureaucracy and 27-month commitment turned us off and sent us back to the Internet.

The scope of one's search must be very wide at the beginning to determine where you want to go, but you also need to know when to drill down into the particulars to avoid spiraling into the Internet's mire. Somewhere along the line, decisions must be made. It takes discipline, dedication and a ton of good fortune to conduct fruitful research without getting stuck in informational quicksand.

The hours flew by as I looked at just about everything Google could throw my way. I sat in the early morning darkness, my coffee growing cold as the sun rose over Marblehead, sifting through blog posts and links to information aggre- gators and downloading PDF documents. Often, realizing how late the hour had become, I would make a dash to the shower, dress and head off to work—my body behind the wheel but my mind thousands of miles away, consumed with whatever tidbit I had encountered in the early hours of the day.

The research was invigorating. It inspired and enticed me. It represented the dangled bauble of freedom and life-changing experience. It began with being inquisitive (which I am, by nature) and nosy (ditto). As a journalist I had learned to pay attention to the follow-up questions to the follow-up questions, as they nearly always elicited the best quotes from the most polished politician, sports hero or business tycoon. I treated myself as an interview subject, and pressed on to find out what made me tick.

I steered clear of voluntourism organizations where fees were high and meaningful cultural experiences were unlikely. I avoided religion-supported volunteer organizations, as the thought of being affiliated with proselytizing or converting had zero appeal.

The Foreign Service wouldn't work, as the daunting application process and buttoned-down government relationship seemed too much like the job I was trying to leave.

I wasn't seeking another career, so work abroad organizations were out of the question.

We considered teaching English abroad, but Gabi and I are both impatient, impulsive and a bit eccentric. We were scared off by the notion of being wed to a schedule and a lesson plan.

We looked for a small, non-sectarian group with a history of excellence and contributions to Southeast Asian society.

Early one morning I discovered the perfect match. San Francisco-based Volunteers in Asia has been placing volunteers throughout Southeast Asia for over 50 years. Small, intimate and with a familial small-organization feel, VIA seemed to perfectly suit our needs. Like other volunteer groups, VIA is a "pay-to-play" organization. Once we completed the application process we plunked down the $2,400 per person fee (that was in 2010; total fees at this writing are now $2,800, including health insurance, program and application fees). We eagerly applied for posts in the following countries (in order):

Thailand
Cambodia
Vietnam
Myanmar

Our application included a notation that while we were unfamiliar with Cambodia, we'd be open to being posted in the country as a "new experience." (We wrote this declaration right before the part in which Gabi listed "impatience in dealing with mundane activities" as a personal weakness. Months later, she would be laboring for hours to edit insufferably long reports, glossaries and other documents littered with the quirky blend of languages we came to know as Khmenglish, thus giving new depths to her understanding of the word "mundane.")

Other volunteer organizations caught my eye, but VIA fit the bill in terms of flexibility (one year with option to renew), support (in-country staff, including language immersion classes) and access to the top dogs in the organization (founder Dwight Clark is still present and active in VIA's activities, and their management and staff are engaged, accessible, supportive and a ton of fun.) With its rich history of sending volunteers to Asian countries, VIA was a proven commodity.

Perfect. We completed the brief application, submitted our CVs, participated in a Skype interview, passed the first stage and were invited to an in-person interview in Washington, DC with two VIA staff members.

Gabi and I flew from Boston and found our way to the meeting at a teahouse in Dupont Circle. We met VIA staffers

Daniel and Anjali tucked away at a second-floor table and had what we thought was a brief, awkward and unfulfilling personal interview with them. Predictable questions elicited perfunctory answers from us, but not a lot of passion. We left the building convinced it had not gone well.

Maybe we weren't a good fit, after all.

Walking away feeling a bit disconsolate, we agreed we would have to search anew for another organization that would take us away from the U.S. into a life of volunteering abroad. We considered going it on our own—moving to Chiang Mai to take a shot at building a life in Southeast Asia.

In early March we received an email from VIA's Southeast Asia program director, Lillian Forsyth: We were in. It was early evening when we received the note, and I was dozing in our seaside condo while Gabi was logged onto her computer. She poked me awake and shared the news.

"Oh, my God … this is really happening!" we shrieked, elated and a bit shocked. We were well on our way to leaving our lives in the U.S. and would be moving to Southeast Asia in three short months.

3
Practical Matters

O*ne Tuesday afternoon in June of 2010, my arms filled with boxes bound for the thrift shop, I was stopped by the man who lived across the street from us. While we'd lived in our rental condo for almost a year, it was the first time he'd spoken to either of us. "Looks like you're moving," he said.*

"Yes, we are," I called back. "Where to?"

I grinned. "Cambodia."

He took a step back. "Wow. Now that's something you don't hear every day."

I'd never fully appreciated how deeply U.S. culture had sunk its hooks into my hide until I began to start to try to disconnect the tethers.

Endless phone calls, letters and certifications were required to cancel telephone, cable TV and banking relationships. Each meeting elicited a similar question: "So, where are you going?" followed by a blank stare and one of two responses when we told them the truth:

"Why would you want to do that?"

... or, much more often:

"I wish I could do something like that."

My conversation with the friendly Comcast rep about cancelling my account set the standard for how amusing the dismounting process had become.

"Hi, Dave (Fred, Sam, or Ted ...). I'm calling to cancel my account.

"OK, Mr. Yetter, but before I process your termination, can I ask why you're cancelling your account? Is there something we can do to keep your business?"

"Well, actually, no; there's nothing you can do. My wife and I are leaving the U.S.

"Oh, wow. Where are you going?

"We're moving to Cambodia next month.

"Wow. Where's that?

"It's near Vietnam.

"Wow. Forhow long?

"We have no idea."

We conferred Power of Attorney rights to a close friend and to my eldest daughter to make sure we could take care of business while out of the country. We had our mail forwarded to a friend to prevent an avalanche of mailings from being sent to our former address.

As we worked through the checklist of what we needed to do to let go, we turned our sights on what we wanted to do to get ready for our new home.

As part of our preparation, we purchased a "Learn the Cambodian language" CD to play in the car while drove around the U.S. on a two-and-a-half month farewell tour, discovering to our horror that the language (Khmer, pronounced K'meye) contained a Sanskrit-based alphabet, could not be Romanized, and contained no punctuation. Khmer script appeared to our baffled eyes as a string of indecipherable scrawls. To our ears, the guttural sound of a recorded native speaker left us overwhelmed. "Roach in my eye," was what my western ears heard when the tape was teaching how to ask a man for his name, "Lok, chmoah aye?" We laughed, gave up and tossed the CD into the back of the car, figuring we'd tackle language training when we got to Cambodia.

Neither of us had ever been to this magical, misunderstood country. We didn't know Cambodia had a seacoast until we began basic researching. I had never known that Phnom Penh, the country's capital, rests at the confluence of the Mekong, Tonle Sap and Bassac rivers, and that the mighty Tonle Sap River changes course once a year, rolling to the north to fill the massive Tonle Sap lake with precious water which provides a home for spawning fish and irrigation for the boundless rice paddies, then south again after the monsoon floods subside. And who knew that the country's second-largest city was Battambang?

Other than having an awareness of the country's tragic history under the Khmer Rouge in the 1970s and the persistent carpet bombing of eastern Cambodia by the U.S. during the Vietnam War, we knew little about the land, culture and people.

As a teenager in the 60s with an emerging sense of social consciousness and a strong disapproval of the war with Vietnam, I spent a fair amount of time plotting an alternative to fighting in the war. The draft was still in effect in my early teens, and although I was eventually issued a draft number, by the time I had received it the draft had been abolished. I was off the hook.

Forty years later, I was doing my best to find a way to move to the region. The irony strikes me even now.

On June 22, 2010, with four suitcases and a ton of ideals, hopes and concerns, we boarded a plane in Boston with one-way tickets to Phnom Penh via Los Angeles and Taipei. We stepped off the ledge of our former lives and while we were excited, thrilled and full of anticipation, these feelings accompanied more than a couple of concerns. I struggled with being so far from my two daughters. We enjoy an understanding with one another built on honestly, openness and patience. I had separated from their mother while my youngest daughter was in high school and we had survived years of awkwardness and challenge as we found ways to forge relationships beyond the "core of four."

Throughout both their college careers I was in constant contact with them, offering (mostly when asked, but occasionally not) advice, guidance, support and editing help with countless papers, predicaments and personal situations. We had always been a phone call away, and rarely did a few days pass before we would exchange a text message or spend a few minutes on the phone to stay connected.

Cambodia would be different. And while I failed to grasp how much technology had shrunk the world (it cost but 20 cents per minute to call my daughters direct from Cambodia over extremely reliable mobile phone connections; the toughest part was figuring out the time difference), I felt the searing pain of a sacrifice I was not sure I wanted to make. Backing out, however, was never an option. Besides, we had entered into this change with our heads up and our eyes wide open.

I'm big on independence and have imbued my daughters with strong senses of self. I celebrate their inherent rights to pursue their lives fully separate from mine. I know they feel the same for me as well as for themselves, but I nonetheless felt a sense of loss.

I had first raised the prospect of living abroad when the four of us were en route to my niece's wedding in southern New Hampshire. Driving north from Boston, I asked them how they would feel if Gabi and I lived in another country. My daughter Kirsty, older and normally more impulsive, was silent. I looked at her in the rear view mirror. I couldn't read the look on her face. Emily, her little sister, spoke first. "Well, dad, I would miss the hell out of you, but I completely understand if this is something you want to do. You've earned it." Our eyes locked in the rear view mirror. I knew she spoke from her heart.

Kirsty chimed in, echoing her sister's sentiments and joining with her to grant me their blessings. It was one of the most important gifts they have given to me; a role reversal of permission, endorsement and acceptance. And, like Gabi's support and encouragement, their unselfish behavior gave license to my wishes.

I felt the separation even before it began. I spoke on the phone with Emily—then a recent graduate of UCLA—while in line at LAX for our flight to Taipei. Choked with tears, I told her I'd be in touch and that we simply would have to find a way to remain connected. It felt very much like a final step.

"It'll be fine, dad," she comforted me, once again turning the tables. "We'll talk. We won't lose touch."

She was right.

That was the personal—and more difficult and important—side of extricating myself from life in the West.

Making the decision to conceptualize and pursue a dream, redraw your life plan, change to a new lifestyle, live in a new country, find a new job or marry a new spouse is as much about breaking free from your diorama as it is about starting work on a new one.

Thinking outside the box sometimes means refusing to live in it. Most of us live in pretty big boxes; ways out seem limited and difficult to find. It's a complicated maze we create for ourselves. My new life began when I realized that more of the same was simply unacceptable. When we left the U.S., it was without a home to return to, cars to drive, furniture to sit on. Thankfully, our family and true friends proved enduring. But we set out with a one-way ticket to Phnom Penh and very few expectations.

This process of emancipation unfolded at glacial speed, yet we were resolved that something had to give.

The analytical/empirical data part of me took charge:

1. Make a list
2. Put stuff on it
3. Check the list
4. Lose the list
5. Create a new list

This zany notion of living somewhere other than in the U.S. started with an entry on a piece of paper. I set forth my life's priorities, drawing upon an idea one of my editors gave me decades ago after I'd taken a pounding from an alert reader who took umbrage over some fact I had either misunderstood, misstated or misrepresented. My ever-alert editor suggested I write a letter to the guy, rip it out of my IBM Selectric, throw it in my desk drawer and forget about it.

So I wrote myself a letter, envisioning what I wanted, cherished, wished for and relished. This time I didn't toss it into my desk drawer (after a career of writing poison-pen letters that were never sent, no room remained in the drawer for as much as a memo scribbled on a cocktail napkin) but kept it on my desk and used it to create and maintain a list of priorities for our next move(s).

1. Quit
2. Think of what to do next
3. Do it
4. Go back to Number 2

This system—manically created over 50+ years and carefully committed to paper over a period of 21 seconds—has served me well. I finally got around to figuring out a formula I could understand and follow.

Planning is anathema to many, including my tumbleweed of a wife. Most of her life was spent following one instinct, urge or impulsive gambit after another. "It's worked out just fine for me," she loves to intone. To a guy who spent 30+ years running in place any path looked attractive.

My expanded short list contained tons of questions and details in each section:

1. Quit: When? How? Who to tell first? What will we live on? How to plan for contingencies? What am I going to worry about when I run out of stuff to put on this list to worry about?

2. Think of what to do next: Throughout my working career I'd given myself headaches trying to brainstorm my next move. Start a business? Be the freelance writer I had once envisioned becoming? Buy a bed and breakfast? Years earlier I had read *What Color is Your Parachute* and decided that I really didn't even have a parachute. I consulted a friend who was professional career coach. His conclusion: "You are technically unemployable," which I took to mean I was either fiercely independent, a self-styled isolationist, or a miserable curmudgeon doomed to a life of occupational solitude.

3. Do it: The tough stuff. I had had a number of "close calls" for serious career changes: as editor of a startup magazine in Massachusetts (financing for the magazine fell through), as publisher of a west-coast weekly newspaper (offer went to someone else), as publisher of my hometown daily newspaper (ditto). None of these cosmetic changes offered the kind of personal overhaul I really wanted.

All the lists, all the thinking, talking, late night hand wringing and exhaustive analysis all led back to the same place: Do it or don't. Much like pregnancy and the inevitability of another member of the Bush family running for president, there's no grey area to making a change like this.

There's no "try" in this equation. "Get busy living or get busy dying."

4

Making the Break

*G*abi sat on the floor in our living room, a tiny stuffed bear with "Gabi" stitched across its chest clutched in her hand. "I can't get rid of this," she said, tears in her eyes. "You bought it for me in Germany."

So it was with the daily challenge to decide what to give away, what to sell, what to donate and what to simply toss.

"My mom gave me this . . . "

"Emily made this for me . . . "

"Remember we bought this in (fill in the blank)?"

"This is Kirsty's . . . ."

Shelves of knickknacks, boxes of books, endless notepads, photo albums and CDs and DVDs became alp-sized obstacles in our quest to simplify, minimize and get ready to leave the U.S..

This *was the hard stuff.*

By nature, my wife and I are more packrats than minimalists, more gatherers than harvesters. She might argue the point, saying she's always lived simply with an eye on flexibility and her next move. But I would invite anyone who buys this line to peek in her handbag. Anyone who carries as much stuff around as Gabi is more tethered to things than perhaps she would admit. As much as we would have liked to think otherwise, we really liked the stuff in our lives: mementoes of our travels, parts of our past lives we had carried into our life as a couple, bicycles, kayaks, golf clubs, cars, and myriad things that go with owning and maintaining a home and living a life of varied interests.

Downsizing—which we did over a year and a half, well before I quit my job and joined VIA, and in two distinct stages—was a challenge to the conventions that had become our lives.

We moved from a three-bedroom, three-bathroom house in Marblehead, Mass., to a two-bedroom 1 ½-bath rented condo nearby. Situated on Marblehead Harbor, the condo hardly constituted "roughing it," but our living space was suddenly reduced to a fraction of the size.

But downsizing can be fun and purifying. And shifting status from "homeowner" to "renter" had many advantages: no lawn to mow (I'm that guy who never had it in him to hire someone to cut my grass, a tribute to my stubbornly Protestant upbringing and infantile and futile commitment to "doing it myself."), no five-year cycle of having the house painted (though I recently got a friendly email reminder from College Pro Painters that it was time for a new coat of paint), no more frantic calls to plumbers when the furnace quit during a blizzard or the hot water heater blew while relatives were visiting.

Free from the mundane management issues that go with home ownership, we were able to turn to the details of extricating ourselves from our lives in the U.S. to whatever would come next.

TALES FROM THE ROAD:
LEAPING HEADLONG INTO A NEW
ADVENTURE: JUNE, 2010

ON JUNE 22, SKIP AND I ARE BOARDING A PLANE TO PHNOM PENH, CAMBODIA. ONE WAY.

WE'VE TALKED ABOUT THIS FOR YEARS: LIVING IN ASIA, EXPERIENCING A NEW CULTURE AND CHANGING OUR LIVES AND IT'S HARD TO BELIEVE IT'S NOW ONLY HOURS AWAY.

WE'RE MOVING TO WORK IN A VOLUNTEER CAPACITY ON A ONE YEAR COMMITMENT BUT WE INTEND STAYING LONGER. WE'VE SOLD OUR HOUSE AND OUR CARS AND EITHER SOLD,

STORED OR GIVEN AWAY ALL OF OUR POSSESSIONS WITH NO INTENTION OF RETURNING ANYTIME SOON.

IT'S SURREAL.

OVER THE PAST WEEKS, I'VE BEEN WORKING OUT IN THE GYM, DRINKING COFFEE WITH A FRIEND OR WALKING THROUGH TOWN WHEN IT SUDDENLY HITS ME WITH A COMBINATION OF DISBELIEF, EXCITEMENT, NERVOUSNESS AND OVERWHELM. IT'S LIKE BUTTERFLIES YOU GET WHEN YOU PERFORM IN A PLAY, COMPETE IN AN EVENT OR GIVE A SPEECH-THE SENSATION OF KNOWING IT WILL TURN OUT FINE BUT REELING FROM THE IMMEDIACY AND ENORMITY OF IT ALL.

I'VE DONE THIS BEFORE. MY LIFE HAS CONSISTED OF MULTIPLE MOVES, MANY TIMES TO COUNTRIES WHERE I KNEW NO-ONE AND HAD VERY LITTLE KNOWLEDGE ABOUT THE PLACE I WOULD LIVE.

MY FAMILY MOVED TO SOUTH AFRICA FROM BAHRAIN WHEN I WAS 16. EVEN THOUGH WE HAD DISTANT FAMILY THERE, WE DIDN'T KNOW ANYONE AND I KNEW VERY LITTLE ABOUT THE COUNTRY. NEXT IT WAS MY UNPLANNED MOVE TO THE U.S., THE END-RESULT OF A "VACATION" WITH A GIRLFRIEND THAT TURNED INTO A PERMANENT MOVE.

THEN THERE WAS THE MOVE TO LONDON (WHERE I KNEW PEOPLE) FOLLOWED BY THE TRANSATLANTIC MOVE TO WASHINGTON DC WHERE I DIDN'T KNOW A SOUL.

EACH TIME FELT LIKE AN ADVENTURE AND THE EXPERIENCE TURNED OUT TO BE PERFECT. SO WHY SHOULD THIS TIME BE ANY DIFFERENT?

THE VERY SAME THINGS WHICH GIVE ME MOMENTS OF PANIC ARE THE SAME WHICH MAKE MY HEART BEAT WITH EXCITEMENT: LEARNING A STRANGE NEW LANGUAGE, MEETING PEOPLE FROM DIFFERENT WALKS OF LIFE, INTEGRATING INTO A NEW CULTURE, EXPLORING THE CITY, FINDING A PLACE TO LIVE.

DISCOVERING WHERE LOCALS EAT AND SHOP, LEARNING HOW TO MANAGE WITHOUT THE FAMILIARITIES OF HOME, WORKING IN AN OFFICE AND COMMUNICATING WITH CAMBODIAN COLLEAGUES.

FIGURING OUT HOW TO GET TO WORK AND HOW TO LIVE WITHOUT TRANSPORTATION. IN THE MEANTIME, HOWEVER, I'VE DISCOVERED SOME NEW TRUTHS:

YOU CAN MANAGE WELL WITH VERY LITTLE "STUFF."

SEPARATION IS HARD AND SOMETIMES IRRATIONAL. EVEN THOUGH WE DECIDED TO GET RID OF OUR CARS, I DIDN'T LIKE THE THOUGHT OF A STRANGER DRIVING AWAY IN MY LITTLE BLACK CONVERTIBLE.

THINGS ONLY HAVE MEANING WHEN YOU ATTACH A MEMORY TO THEM. OUR IRISH ANTIQUE HUTCH WAS A GREAT PIECE OF FURNITURE BUT WHAT MADE IT REALLY SPECIAL WAS THE MEMORY OF HOW WE FOUND IT TUCKED

AWAY IN A EUROPEAN IMPORT STORE AND PLACED IT IN THE FIRST HOME SKIP AND I BOUGHT TOGETHER.

THERE'S AN INCREDIBLE POIGNANCY IN SEEING THINGS FOR WHAT MAY BE THE LAST TIME: THE BOATS ON THE HARBOR, THE MOON SHINING ON THE OCEAN OUTSIDE OUR WINDOW, MY CAT CURLED UP ON THE BED. IT'S WHEN YOU LEAVE THAT YOU NOTICE DIFFERENT QUALITIES IN YOUR FRIENDS. I'VE OBSERVED HOW SOME MADE THEMSELVES MORE ABSENT WHILE MOST OF OUR TRUE FRIENDS PERSISTENTLY GRABBED EVERY OPPORTUNITY TO GET TOGETHER.

THIS ISN'T A RATIONAL FEELING, IT COMES FROM THE PIT OF MY STOMACH-THE PLACE WHICH SPEAKS TO ME IN THE MIDDLE OF THE NIGHT AND GRABS ME BY THE THROAT, CAUSING MY HEART TO BEAT FAST AND MY PALMS TO GROW SWEATY. IT'S ABOUT TRANSITION AND LETTING GO.

AND I KNOW THAT, ONCE WE PASS THROUGH THE SECURITY GATE WITH OUR SUITCASES AND PASSPORTS IN HAND, ARMED WITH OUR CAMBODIA HANDBOOKS AND KHMER LANGUAGE TAPES, I WILL NOT LOOK BACK.

SO FOR NOW, I WANT TO SAVOR EVERY MOMENT, EVERY EXPERIENCE, EVERY TIDE AND FULL MOON AND TIME WITH FRIENDS.

i WANT TO WATCH THE EXPRESSIONS ON PEOPLE'S FACES AND OBSERVE THE BEAUTY OF BOUGAINVILLEA BLOOMING IN OUR NEIGHBOR'S GARDEN. i WANT TO SIT QUIETLY WITH MY CAT, GRACIE ON MY LAP AND BREATHE DEEPLY DURING THIS FLURRY OF ACTIVITY.

WE WILL SOON BE ARRIVING IN A NEW WORLD WITH EXCITING NEW EXPERIENCES, STARTING A NEW CHAPTER IN OUR LIVES, BUT i KNOW THIS STAGE WILL BE FOREVER ETCHED IN MY MEMORY.

iT WILL SIGNIFY A PERIOD WHEN WE DECIDED iT WAS TIME TO MAKE A CHANGE. WHEN, NO MATTER HOW CONTENT WE WERE, WE'D DECIDED TO LET GO OF THE TRAPEZE AND GRAB FOR THE NEXT SWINGING BAR; HEADED TO A PLACE WHERE WE KNOW NOBODY, DON'T SPEAK THE LANGUAGE AND HAVE NO KNOWLEDGE OF THE COUNTRY.

iT'S OUR ADVENTURE WAITING TO BEGIN.

5
Moving: From Here to There

I separated myself from the conversation at a friend's cocktail party and moved to the bar, where the bartender refreshed my glass with another couple of fingers of Chardonnay. I felt a hand on my elbow and turned to encounter a woman who has been a friend for over 30 years.

"What's this I hear about you quitting your job and moving across the world?" she asked, her eyes glimmering with the prospect of discovering just how completely I'd lost my mind.

"Yeah, it's true. We're bagging it all and moving to Cambodia."

"Cambodia! But why? And what about your job? Are they going to hold it open for you? A sabbatical?"

"Nope. I'm quitting."

"Are you nuts? Half this room would give their right eyeballs for a shot at your job. And you're young, what, just over 50?"

"Yeah, it's a great job, and the company's been good to me. But I'm done with it."

"What about your kids?"

"Actually, they're among our biggest supporters?"

"And Gabi?"

"Well, duh...."

"What about your grandchildren? How could you move so far away from family?

"Jeez, maybe you know something I don't, but the last time I checked neither of my daughters is married or with child."

Selling the house was an expensive but necessary step—the castor oil of our quest for independence. We'd bought our home at the height of the suburban Boston area housing market and sold as the housing valuation slide began to pick up speed. This loss hurt, and it cut painfully into our nest egg, but it was an important step, after which we were unable to turn back.

Selling the house meant a dramatic reduction of personal responsibilities, a crucial step toward emancipation.

With home sales taking longer and lending requirements becoming tighter, we felt lucky to find a qualified buyer. We jumped at the opportunity to take the loss. We hadn't bought our home as an investment but as a great place to live and an important tax deduction. Since our plan to dismount from life in the U.S. included a quick trip from the top of the tax bracket to the bottom, our need for a tax deduction became about as pressing as our need for three bedrooms. Empty nesters with big houses only end up heating unoccupied rooms.

We had been in the home for less than five years. When we bought our home, we chose one of the noxious, interest-only ARM loans that ended up crushing many consumers, but it made financial sense at the time. Now, however, it looked pretty grim: We faced a higher mortgage payment as housing values plummeted.

Decision time: Either refinance (and recommit to earning an ongoing income to pay the mortgage) or sell.

Sell.

No way was I going to start over with a mortgage of 10, 15 or 30 years, though I knew we could afford it, and a new financial commitment wouldn't affect us dramatically. But at that point in my life it would have been like starting a new family. As much as I adore my daughters, changing diapers and cleaning Cheerios out of the back seat of my car is the kind of experience I wanted to have only twice in life.

Once we signed the P&S, we faced the daunting task of getting rid of our stuff. We needed a disciplined approach to shedding the countless layers of skin that go with suburban life. After a brief spell of serious anguish, the goal became simple: reduce, simplify, give it away to someone who needs or wants it and try not to hold onto stuff that had emotional appeal but little practical relevance.

We stumbled over things that had emotional value, but once we hit stride it was like running downhill. Simplifying our lives meant purification; the purge was a gateway to what lay ahead. We dug into the details of breaking our bonds with the U.S. to set up life in another part of the world. I needed another checklist:

1. Quit job: Check.
2. Close bank accounts: Check.
3. Cancel landline phone, cable TV, Boston Globe home delivery, gym membership, Verizon Wireless account: Check (the thrill of this particular act, which brought closure to a long, uncomfortable relationship, tickles me to this day).
4. Review terms of health insurance offered through Volunteers in Asia: Check.
5. Contact bank in Cambodia to find out about opening an account there: Check.
6. Start learning conversational Khmer: In progress, thanks to in-home lessons by Thary Sun Lim, a Cambodian friend of my daughter who exhibited tremendous patience by helping us over some of the rudimentary basics in our living room.
7. Make plans to say goodbye to people.

As we worked through the list of stuff to do everything went smoothly and according to our western-trained minds, even setting up a bank account in Phnom Penh.

Very simple, said the bank officer with whom I exchanged several email messages as part of our preparation to leave for Cambodia. Just bring cash or a bank draft, come into one of our branches with a valid passport and a "letter of endorsement" from the non-governmental organization you are working for, and we'll set up your account right away.

His email detailed the nature of banking in Cambodia: what they would require, deposit rules, ATM accessibility, etc., but I was a bit shocked with his response about the limits on transferring funds from one country to another: "I personally moved to Cambodia from the U.S.A back in 2007," he wrote. "I brought my savings with me which amounted to U.S. $25,000. I had no trouble! Of course, I didn't declare." Standard language on most arrival forms limits the amount of money one can bring into a country to $10,000.

In the wild west of Phnom Penh, money talks and rules are not so much made to be broken as they are to be ignored.

I'm a "by the books" kind of guy, so I elected to bring a decent wad of cash to set up the account. Then I could wire funds into the account as needed. I paid wire transfer fees on both ends of the transaction, but this turned out to be the simplest and most reliable method of keeping cash on hand.

Setting up the bank account was easy once we were in Cambodia. Meeting with an English-speaking service rep in a clean, neatly pressed uniform, I provided a copy of my passport, a letter from the NGO I was working for verifying my "employment," and we were good to go. They set up online banking and issued an ATM card emblazoned with my photo on the back to help protect against theft and fraud (what a great idea!)

Once we were liquid and armed with a local bank's ATM card, we discovered how small the world had become in terms of bank access. There are loads of places in Cambodia where you won't find many ATMs (such as the popular coastal towns of Kep and Kampot) but you get used to loading up with cash before you hit the road.

The rest of our new life presented countless obstacles and challenges, but rolling with the unexpected punches became de rigueur. We learned that etching our day's expectations in stone only meant we'd be seriously disappointed before lunchtime.

I look on our first three years of living abroad as an educational experience. Now I possess a Master's Degree in Living in Tumult, and am pursuing a Ph.D. in Figuring Stuff Out in Places where I am Clueless. There's no course syllabus for Cambodia, no Cliff's Notes version, though there are a ton of willing, able and capable instructors. After three-and-a-half years learning the ways of life in Cambodia, here's what I know about how the country works: *Nothing*. Zero. The more I think I know, the more I am reminded that I still have no clue what's going on around me. Cambodia is a place where yes often means no, a smile during a casual disagreement is a sign of growing discomfort, and a display of anger only discredits you to the point where you will no longer be relevant to the conversation.

It took some getting used to, and some serious attitude adjustment.

I spoke enough Khmer to handle myself in most situations, but I also developed an auditory filter that I could switch on and off. This permitted me to live in a bubble of relative silence and peace, isolated from what the locals were jabbering about while very much in public. I came to like it that way.

Now I have a hard time in places where I'm able to dissect the banter from nearby tables and endless assault of marketing messages from all around. During trips to the U.S. and UK, I experience mild headaches when we are in public places because I can not only hear the people around me, I can understand them. It's confounding, as if I've contracted a form of cultural Attention Deficit Disorder.

We stepped off the plane on June 22, 2010 into a city of 1.4 million people who all maniacally circled the dusty streets on motorbikes or in cars, trucks or *tuk-tuks* (a simple local taxi consisting of a motorbike pulling a covered four-seat metal wagon). Many sat by the side of the road waiting for something to happen. Some drove on the wrong side of the streets, ignoring stop signs and street lights and dodging police who would step into the road, waving red and white batons in an effort to force drivers to the side of the road to shake them down for a few dollars of "fines."

Our friend Ramon, once confronted on his motorbike by a cop who stepped into the road in an attempt to stop him, yanked the frantically waving red and white baton from the policeman's hands as he swerved around him. (Not recommended for travel novices, but it's a good story and an example of the wild nature of Phnom Penh's streets.)

The initial shock of living in a hot, dusty and stinky place (our first impressions) where the food, language and way of living was unlike anything we had experienced often left us huddling in our tiny air-conditioned room at the $10 per night guest lodge where VIA housed us. Sidewalks ended abruptly in piles of rubble, forcing us into street traffic. Vendors pushed carts everywhere, loaded with heaping bowls of stuff that looked not only inedible but as though it had been lying around for days in a mass of coagulating fat.

VIA wisely planned three weeks of orientation and indoctrination. To dump us into a city without a well-thought integration process would have been beyond chaotic. Had we gone completely on our own, I'm not sure the ending would have played out as it did.

Every morning we ventured forth with our fellow volunteers like nervous mice from our burrows. Sweating from the moment we stepped into the humidity, we would buy the first of the day's endless liters of filtered water and set out for language class. We'd break for lunch, commiserate with our colleagues over the difficulty of learning Khmer while trying to figure out where to live and get ready to start our volunteer positions. After dinner, while once again sweating through our shirts, we retreated to our guesthouse rooms to cool down, reconnect and plot our next moves.

One night while walking back from dinner, we encountered an enormous rat that scampered across the road into a pile of garbage slightly smaller than Mt. Washington. I tried to divert Gabi's attention, thinking the appearance of beagle-sized vermin could well be the final prompt for her to book a return flight to the U.S., UK or anywhere unlike Cambodia. I failed to distract her, she recoiled in predictable fashion, and we spent a chunk of the evening reviewing how we felt about this place and whether it was truly for us.

My wife: Beautiful, gentle and eternally positive and friendly, she is often underestimated by those who fail to see the tiger within her. She is at once tough and vulnerable, quiet and outspoken, indecisive and driven, but unwaveringly resilient.

I've watched in awe as Gabi rolled up her pants legs and waded through knee-deep filthy water in India. I've seen her wipe the sweat out of her eyes and reach for the next branch while ascending a steep path on a hike in Costa Rica. I've witnessed her struggling down the side of a mountain in northern Thailand as thick smoke from a nearby brush fire impeded our view during a morning hike in the hills. But after watching her labor for days—grappling more than me with the chaotic wackiness that is Phnom Penh—I wondered whether we would begin searching for an apartment or planning an exit.

It all changed, as do many challenges, after a good night's sleep, a long talk and the introduction to the first of Phnom Penh's countless air-conditioned coffee shops. Having discovered an oasis of calm, cool and good coffee, we were free to investigate and learn about our new home.

We also benefitted from our network of colleagues and from the support staff at VIA. The health insurance, language training and connections to the non-government organizations we were working for were all invaluable, but the calm, understanding support of colleagues who understood what we were feeling was the foundation upon which we built our new life.

Life in Phnom Penh was an interesting dynamic. We were in our 50s with a wealth of life and work experience tethered to reality by a group of 20-year-olds who had much more time and experience on the ground in Southeast Asia. They were our lifelines and guides, and proved tireless advocates for us to seek, explore, challenge, accept and keep moving forward. Moving forward: That's why we were here. Inertia had held us on the same course for many years; we had made a conscious decision to leave behind the life, stuff and predictability of what we had in the U.S. for something different.

Each day presented us with a new set of challenges, new opportunities to learn—new obstacles that would push our buttons and our patience to the limit. It was stimulating, invigorating, frustrating, and enormous fun. Every day was different. We had so many "Wow!" moments we began to lose track of them. Within weeks, we began to develop a numbness to the shock of living in a developing country.

We lived our first month under the careful guidance of VIA staff who patiently escorted us about the city, introduced us to language training and answered endless questions about where to go, what to buy, how to do and the insiders' details that go with setting up shop in a new place.

To our surprise, we found a number of things that actually worked better than in the States. ATMs proved more ubiquitous than in the U.S.; they rank alongside cell phone reception as superior to what I experienced in the West. (Despite living in Boston, one of the U.S.'s top technology corridors, I experienced more dropped calls there than I care to remember. After threeplus years in Cambodia, I never experienced a dropped call … even from the middle of rice paddies and rural provinces on my bicycle. I'd sit astride my mountain bike in Kandal Province chattering away with one of my daughters on the phone. Four years earlier, I couldn't finish a conversation with my sales manager while driving the 18 miles from Marblehead to Boston without hitting a dead spot and losing the call.)

Since hitting the road, we've collected SIM cards as we've traveled from Cambodia through Asia, Western Europe, Cyprus, Turkey and Greece. Mobile phone service is better, cheaper and more reliable just about anywhere outside the U.S.

TALES FROM THE ROAD: WE'RE HERE, BUT WE'RE NOT ALL THERE
JUNE, 2010

IT'S FRIDAY MORNING. WE'VE BEEN HERE FOR LESS THAN 24 HOURS AND I'M STRUGGLING TO FIND THE WORDS TO EXPLAIN HOW IT FEELS. OUR INITIAL ARRIVAL TOOK US INTO A SPARSE AIRPORT WHERE WE WERE WHISKED THROUGH

DISEMBARKATION, VISA APPLICATION AND BAG DELIVERY IN AN IMPRESSIVE 20 MINUTES. THE TUK-TUK FROM THE SPRING GUEST HOUSE WAS WAITING FOR US.

WE LOADED ALL OUR BAGS INTO THE BACK OF THE VEHICLE AND TOOK OFF-INTO SOMETHING I'VE NEVER QUITE EXPERIENCED BEFORE: DIRTY ROADS, WILD DRIVERS, LACK OF ANY SYSTEM OF TRAFFIC CONTROL, BROKEN DOWN BUILDINGS, STIFLING HEAT AND A FEELING OF BEING SO COMPLETELY OUT OF MY ELEMENT THAT I AM NOT SURE HOW TO DEAL WITH IT.

IT'S FUNNY HOW A CONCEPT IS SOMETIMES VERY DIFFERENT FROM REALITY; I WONDER IF I GLAMORIZED THE IDEA OF PHNOM PENH WITHOUT REALLY LEARNING ENOUGH ABOUT WHAT I WAS COMING TO. I'D IMAGINED A SOPHISTICATED, WORLDLY CITY WHERE WE COULD GET MOST OF THE THINGS WE HAVE AT HOME, FIND NICE RESTAURANTS AND WALK THROUGH INTERESTING STREETS.

INSTEAD, I AM EXPERIENCING A PLACE THAT IS NOTHING OF THE KIND. THE STREETS ARE CHAOTIC AND IT'S IMPOSSIBLE TO CROSS THE ROAD WITHOUT LINGERING ON THE EDGE TO HOLD YOUR BREATH AS MOTORBIKES, TUK-TUKS, CARS, BICYCLES AND STREET VENDORS WHIZ BY IN A SENSELESS MESS OF DISORDER AND CONFUSION. MOST OF

THE TIME, SKIP GRABS MY HAND AND YANKS ME BEHIND HIM. OTHERWISE, WE'D STAND FOR HOURS WAITING FOR A BREAK IN THE ACTION.

THE SIDEWALKS ARE BROKEN UP AND FILLED WITH GARBAGE. EVERYTHING STINKS. THE HEAT IS STIFLING AND I'M CONSTANTLY DAMP FROM HEAD TO TOE. THERE ARE CHICKENS ON THE STREET. NOTHING IS SOPHISTICATED. NOTHING IS CUTE. IT IS INCREDIBLY OVERWHELMING, SCARY AND WEIRD.

IT'S HARD FOR ME TO IMAGINE BEING HERE FOR 12 DAYS, NEVER MIND 12 MONTHS.

AS EXPECTED, OUR SURROUNDINGS ARE UNFAMILIAR. AS A BACKPACKER HOTEL, I'M SURE IT'S FINE, BUT AFTER THE LUXURY OF EVA AIR, WE NOW FIND OURSELVES IN A 12' BY 14' TILED ROOM WITH A DOUBLE BED, A TINY BEDSIDE TABLE WITH A PHONE, A SMALL DRESSER CONTAINING A 12" TV, ONE HANGER FOR CLOTHES AND TWO DRAWERS (GUESS WE'LL BE LIVING OUT OF SUITCASES FOR 4 WEEKS). THE BATHROOM HAS A SHOWER BUT THE SHOWER ACTUALLY IS THE BATHROOM AS THERE'S A HANDHELD SHOWERHEAD ON THE WALL. YOU HAVE TO SHOWER IN THE MIDDLE OF THE ROOM, WITH NO CURTAIN, NO DOOR OR NO TUB. YES, THE BATHROOM IS ALWAYS WET! (AND THE SOAP THEY PROVIDED WAS MISTAKEN BY SKIP WHO THOUGHT IT WAS A mint on our pillow-one of our funnier moments).

THEN, AS WE WALKED into THE GUESTHOUSE AROUND 11 PM, A RAT RAN ACROSS OUR PATHS.

TODAY, WE WERE BOTH FULLY AWAKE AT 5AM, AFTER 4 1/2 HOURS SLEEP, SO DECIDED TO VENTURE OUT. WE WALKED FOR 40 minutes TRYING TO FIND THE AIR-CONDITIONED COFFEE SHOP WE'D SPOTTED LAST NIGHT AND FINALLY GAVE UP, HAILING AN EVER-PRESENT TUK-TUK, AND LETTING HIM GUIDE US TO A SIMILAR SPOT WHERE WE FOUND ICED LATTES (SOMEWHAT SWEETER THAN THOSE AT HOME), CROISSANTS AND AIR CONDITIONING.

AS WE PLAYED CARDS AND REMINISCED ABOUT THE PATH in our lives WHICH HAD LED US HERE, WE DECIDED WE COULD ALWAYS FIND LITTLE OASES ALONG THE WAY, PLACES WHERE WE COULD TAKE REFUGE in THE FAMILIAR WHENEVER WE NEED THEM: ICED LATTES, FOOT MASSAGES, AIR-CONDITIONING, AMERICAN PROGRAMS on TV, LUXURY HOTEL ROOMS.

IT IS IMPORTANT TO GO ONE STEP AT A TIME. BREATHE, TALK TO ONE ANOTHER, REALIZE WE HAVE CHOSEN TO BE HERE. THERE IS NOTHING WE CAN'T DO TOGETHER WHEN WE HAVE THE RIGHT OUTLOOK.

JUST, PLEASE, PLEASE, PLEASE: NO MORE RATS.

6

Contrasts: Then and Now

"*Remember how Sunday mornings used to be about pancakes at Mildred's Diner and getting for work on Monday?*" *said Gabi, as dozens of Cambodian and Vietnamese teenagers poured through the door of our Phnom Penh apartment shortly after 7 a.m. I wiped the sweat from my face while I fried pounds of bacon and scrambled dozens of eggs in our cramped kitchen. Our living room quickly filled with students from an organization run by a friend that provides cross-cultural training for young adults representing two populations who traditionally have shared deeply embedded hatred. One of one of the students picked up my guitar and began to strum it. Another ran into the kitchen, eager to learn how to prepare a western breakfast.*

Within the next 60 minutes, we'd prepared hearty meals for 25 people, not a morsel of food remained, and all the plates and cooking equipment had been cleaned and put away.

As they thanked us, hugged us and marched out the door to the day's adventures, Gabi and I glowed with happiness. The day had hardly begun, and already we felt a tremendous sense of personal accomplishment and happiness over feeding our new expanded family. Mildred's Diner had never felt like this.

This chapter offers a snapshot of our lives in two parts, the first a profile of our "prior lives" living and working in the U.S., the second our lives as we came to know them.

Marblehead and Boston, Mass., 2009

I am a simple guy of durable stock, raised with traditional ideals. Born in western Massachusetts in the mid-1950s to a florist and a nurse, the path of my life seemed pretty straightforward: go to school, get a job, work your tail off, raise a family, join the consumer marathon race, buy and sell a house or two, retire, golf, relax, die.

I married and divorced twice and had two daughters by my second marriage, which ended after 22 years. Gabi was a friend and colleague whom I had known for years. We fell in love, and after a lengthy long-distance relationship (she in London, me in the U.S.) married and began a fresh, new life together.

Somewhere along the line it became clear that I had horribly oversimplified—or wholly misunderstood—the rules of engagement for life in the U.S. I began to question it all as I felt the malaise of discontentment, the persistent tug at one's heartstrings that comes with wondering what else might be out there.

I had followed a traditional path after a tumultuous adolescence in the 1960s and 70s, journalism school in university, an entry level job for a daily newspaper in western Mass., promotions, job changes, marriage/divorce, blah, blah, blah. With some personal side journeys, I followed a fairly predictable path of life.

As a fledgling reporter, I encountered all sorts of people with different modes of living, different rules: anarchists, poets, musicians, politicians, murderers, New Age idealists, New Deal reactionaries and a gazillion just plain folks who were doing their time on the treadmill just like me. I became attracted to people who were different—the man who had accumulated dozens of U.S. patents inventing things, the immigrant laborer who became a Golden Gloves boxing champ and counseled troubled inner city youths, the host of a popular TV nature show who, at 86, humbled me with his energy as we climbed to a mountain peak to chronicle the recovery of a peregrine falcon colony.

I envied these people from a comfortable distance as a reporter, then years later as a businessman far removed from the rigors of a beat reporter. Casual contact with people like these imbued me with a sense of envy in my early years, then developed into a focused effort to make my life more like theirs.

The final chapter of my work life consisted of 40+ hours a week behind a desk overlooking City Hall Plaza in downtown Boston. I was in charge of global sales for Business Wire, a wonderful company owned by Warren Buffet and Berkshire Hathaway. I faced a 90-minute commute each morning, less on the way home if I planned my exit properly, and tried to balance the demands of managing the sales efforts of staff in a couple dozen offices around the world with time in the gym to break up the day.

Gabi worked from home for New York-based Medialink, selling video production services to New England-based companies until a corporate reorganization eliminated her job. She began her own business selling a self-designed specialty item online and continued to work from home.

We golfed a lot, dined out, entertained, traveled and spent time with my family and our friends in New England and with her family in England.

It was a rich, busy and generous lifestyle that nonetheless left us feeling increasingly empty, me more than Gabi. Hence my evolving disdain for Sunday afternoons.

Like squaring off with the taxman each April 15 or performing any unseemly but required task, work for me was like a mandatory college freshman course: boring as hell, but no way around it. While in college I slept through English 101, but even an accomplished bullshitter like me couldn't somnambulate my way through the American workplace. I became a master of avoidance, along the way developing considerable skills to repress my unhappiness with a life full of stuff, experiences and things to fill the time. Going to work became a routine of perfunctory exercises mostly designed to pass the hours. Time off was a brief respite in between forced marches.

This wasn't clinical depression, nor job dissatisfaction or general malaise. Over the years I had uncovered a spiritual and emotional void that simply would not go away.

That Monday morning in January 2010 when I finally quit my job was my turning point.

Family was supportive; friends more mixed. One fairly close friend said she thought I was nuts. "You've left a job working for one of the world's greatest companies at the top of your earning potential to do what? Volunteer? Live abroad? Are you insane?"

Insane, no. Awake and aware? You bet.

I had looked around at some point in my daily step onto the treadmill and didn't recognize the view. As 2009 drew to a close I realized that everything in my life had changed.

My parents had both passed away. My kids were grown and moved away. There was a lot of emptiness in a big house full of stuff. I had quit my job and cut a gaping hole in my safety net and Gabi and I often asked ourselves, "What's next?"

Time for a change.

Where did this come from?

Our one-way stroll into Something Very Different had begun in 2007, when we visited Thailand on our honeymoon.

Phnom Penh and Southeast Asia, 2010-2013

Three years after honeymooning in Thailand, we sunk our roots in Cambodia, first as volunteers for two non-governmental organizations; me, working with a small Cambodian NGO that lobbied the government on economic policy regarding the development of oil, gas and mining in the country; Gabi, providing English resource support to a large NGO that provided training to the country's rural population.

We were on foreign turf with little experience to guide us. But we were happy, fulfilled, challenged and stimulated beyond description.

With a two-bedroom rental apartment in the heart of Phnom Penh as a base, Gabi and I spent days providing English language support and our free time exploring Southeast Asia.

We didn't own our home, a car, or much of anything.

In Cambodia, we earned a combined $740 a month in our volunteer jobs, made extra money through freelance writing

(Gabi) and business consulting (me) and supplemented our income with carefully managed draws against our savings. Our life was stubbornly minimalist and devoid of possessions but abundant in enriching experiences.

Like a pair of butterflies released from our cocoons of duty and obligation in the U.S., we fell into a life of exploration and cultural and social experiences that broadened our thinking, challenged our conventions and fueled our fire for more. We dove into a rigorous daily program of living Khmer life, culture, food and language, hopelessly over our heads but relishing the challenges and how alive it all made us feel.

Being in unfamiliar circumstances became the norm. And four years into this massive change of life, we're addicted to it. We see no end to it, and that's perfectly fine with us.

In August 2013, we made another major move. We left Cambodia, travelled through Asia for four months then spent most of the following year housesitting throughout Europe. From here, our life horizon looks pretty much the same: Unplanned and unknown.

How did this radical change come about? It started with me looking myself in the eye and answering one of the toughest questions I've faced: *What do you want to do with the rest of your life?*

Typical of our marital behavior, Gabi and I took different approaches to our new lives.

Gabi's Story

I've always been an online research junkie so when we moved to Phnom Penh I started with LinkedIn, which I've belonged to for many years. I looked up all the Cambodian groups (such as Cambodia Business Network, Cambodia Professionals, Cambodia Private Sector and Cambodia Creative Hub) and joined them all. I skimmed the listings of every member of each list and picked some who sounded interesting or had similar backgrounds to Skip or me. Through LinkedIn, I sent personal emails introducing myself, explaining we were new in town and mentioning we were keen to know more about life in Phnom Penh if they were open to meeting for coffee or lunch. I received replies from most. Some didn't pan out; others became friends.

I posted queries or information of my own when I had something to share. One was about a volunteer position I'd been approached about from a local organization and was unable to do myself. After posting it on LinkedIn I received an inquiry from a woman in the U.S. who was planning on moving to Phnom Penh to be closer to her son in Hong Kong. She ended up getting the job. I chatted regularly with her online while she was planning her move, provided her with information about the city, offered to meet her at the airport and ended up becoming online—and then actual—friends.

On a non-virtual level and through "old fashioned" networking, I found out about social groups in Phnom Penh—the British Chamber of Commerce, Women's International Group, American Chamber of Commerce, Phnom Penh Toastmasters— and went along to some of their events. I didn't become a member of any but they offered another way to meet people and figure out who we might want to include in our social circle.

We found it easier to meet people and make friends in an expat community than we had back home. People weren't as wrapped up in their own circle of friends, clubs, churches or school groups. Instead, we were all in the same boat—living in a country that wasn't our home and keen to meet like-minded individuals who spoke the same language. Social appointments were made faster than back home and relationships formed quickly.

For example, we bumped into our downstairs neighbor on the staircase less than a week after we moved in and struck up a conversation in the stairway. "Let's get together for a drink sometime," we suggested. "How about tonight?" he replied.

Back home, it would never have worked that way. He'd first have to consult his wife. We'd all check our diaries, make sure we had no other plans, then schedule something for a date, perhaps two or three weeks away, which might just as likely get postponed or canceled.

Since there's a large NGO community in Phnom Penh, many westerners move to Cambodia for periods of time, anywhere from three months to three years. Expats working in corporate positions bring their families along for a few years. Backpackers and voyagers arrive in the country, fall in love with it and decide to prolong their stays by finding volunteer work, teaching English or getting a temporary job. Our friends included all of the above. They came from Australia, England, New Zealand, the U.S, The Netherlands, France, Italy and Canada so we were a wonderfully mixed and motley crew.

We also found social outings to be more, well, social. Friends invited us along when they were going to a picnic or a dinner party. In turn, we'd tell our friends to bring people with them when they came to our home instead of restricting evenings to just the four of us. One year, we hired a boat on the river for Thanksgiving, invited a handful of friends and told them to invite other people for a giant turkey potluck. We'd make instant connections with people we met in coffee shops or on the street and invite them to dinner or to join us for quiz night or an evening at the movie house. Our social circle broadened rapidly.

My freelance writing work offered another way to meet people. Through articles I wrote for local online publications (*Khmer440, Expat Advisory, Latitudes*), I created introductions

to people I wanted to meet. Ramon Stoppelenburg, who I interviewed when he bought the local movie house, became one of
our close friends. Laura Snook, who was editor of *Southeast
Asia Globe* (a regional magazine I wrote for) became another, as
did Ruth Larwill, another interview subject and the owner of
Bloom (a fabulous bakery and social enterprise, conveniently
located on our street). Phil and Ritchy, a couple of locally famous
French jazz musicians, invited us to their events as did one of the
Cambodian Princesses, Soma Norodom, who I met at a Phnom
Penh Academy Awards party I wrote about.

I attended classes or seminars that were of interest: a photography class, a seminar on personal growth, the Phnom Penh
TedX conference, an apsara dance class. Many were one-offs
but I sometimes met someone I wanted to see again (or introduce to my husband) so I'd always get a business card and
drop them a note within a day or two suggesting coffee or
a cocktail.

We became part of the online community of Phnom Penh
through the Yahoo group, Cambodian Parents' Network (not
only for parents and the best resource for finding anything in
Phnom Penh, whether it's knowing where to buy good quality shoes, where to stay on a weekend jaunt to the neighboring
islands or how to fairly compensate employees). On the CPN

group, I learned about a newly developing book club (which I joined and made a couple of friends through), heard about a movie club (that I attended twice before it fizzled out) and read about an organization that needed a writer for their newsletter (I applied and got the job).

The more visible I made myself, the more I became part of the community. The more I became part of the community, the more I was able to help new arrivals in Cambodia find their feet and locate jobs, opportunities or neighborhoods to live in. People contacted me online for help when they were moving to (or visiting) Phnom Penh. In turn, I introduced newcomers to people who might be helpful for them and continued to broaden my circle.

The (unintended) benefits included more paying work. One of our friends heard of an opportunity to write a chapter in a book about moving to Southeast Asia and provided me with an introduction to the publisher. I ended up getting the assignment, which evolved from a single chapter into an entire book *(The Definitive Guide to Moving to Southeast Asia: Cambodia)*. An online contact recommended me to write the newsletter for their non-profit organization, and a large French NGO discovered me online and hired me to write a book on traditional Cambodian desserts for their fund-raising efforts (The Sweet Tastes of Cambodia).

Living overseas as an expat means you fit into a unique niche if you can write. In Phnom Penh (as in many cities), there are many print and online publications, all of which need to fill their pages. They don't pay much but if you can survive on a small income, write a lot of articles or want to supplement your salary, there's always someone who'll buy your articles. I fit into the last category and, since I had plenty of time on my hands, I wrote restaurant reviews, personality profiles, human interest stories and travel pieces that provided a way of meeting some very special people and learning more about the country where I lived.

Skip's story

Gabi is the masterful networker in our partnership—the keeper of the social calendar and the primary advocate of expanding our social network around the things we love to do outside of work: eat, exchange ideas with smart people, experience new things, explore.

I am a more pedestrian networker, my straight-line orientation urging me in search of friends to mountain bike, talk politics over a beer, or hang out at our house over one of my home-cooked meals.

My contacts at work rewarded me richly by opening up deep personal relationships with several Cambodian natives. Those friendships opened unexpected doors for work opportunities. What started with chance meetings and casual conversations quickly became talks about consulting jobs that took on a viral quality as my name got around from satisfied clients.

Consulting turned out to be both lucrative and fun, as I was able to use my business skills and management experience to help numerous Phnom Penh organizations. Unlike in the U.S., where I would have been perceived as an aged and expensive commodity, in Cambodia I was viewed as a source of experience and knowledge for which clients were willing to pay.

My life was far from being about work. My love of mountain biking led me to Phnom Penh's best bike shop and into a chance meeting with a young cycling guide named Buntry Hout. I hired Buntry to show me routes and rides into the provinces of Cambodia, met a handful of fellow bikers with whom I explored some of the out of the way spots around Phnom Penh, and made buddies with the guys who ran the bike shop and kept my bike in working order.

As middle-aged white people, Gabi and I received special treatment and had access to people and places closed to many. After befriending a tuk-tuk driver named Oeurn in the coastal community of Kep, we were delighted when he interrupted our tour of the countryside by taking us to his home to meet his wife and daughter, then climbed to the top of a palm tree to retrieve fresh coconuts for our afternoon refreshment.

The preferential treatment was humbling and at times embarrassing.

At work-related conferences, we were ushered to the front of the room to serve as prestigious props for the TV cameras. At the annual Water Festival, there was a special section for foreigners *(baraing)* cordoned off at a prime viewing spot to watch the riverboat races. We were always embarrassed by the fuss, but got to meet many high-ranking officials and other interesting people simply because we were westerners.

As a middle-aged man in Cambodia, I found it a challenge to meet like-minded people. I didn't relate to the hard-drinking crowd or the upscale expat husband, wasn't interested in frequenting bars to meet friends and didn't want to mix in social circles or join business groups. Little by little, through personal contacts or work connections, I found a small group of guys who had similar mindsets, comparable outlooks and the same love for the simple life in Cambodia. Some of them, I know, will be in my life forever.

Many times during our three years in Cambodia, we felt a bit forgotten. We often talked about the price we might have paid for moving across the world.

We used email and Facebook liberally, and wrote regular group messages to more than 100 friends and family members. Sometimes, we only heard back from two or three.

We posted photos and updates on Facebook and kept a regular blog (www.TheMeanderthals.com) where we both wrote about experiences and adventures in Cambodia. We Skyped with family whenever the mood struck us. We made phone calls to friends when we felt the need to reach out (sometimes calling them in the middle of the night when we miscalculated the time difference). But there were many times when we felt we'd lost touch with people we cared about.

"Remember, you're the ones who left," said one of our friends. "It's not that we don't care. It's just that we are living our lives." There were sacrifices. I missed precious time with my daughters, sisters, nieces and nephews. Nine children came into my family while we lived away, and some friends fell by the wayside as we changed and moved on. While it hurt to know we'd lost some of our friends, we discovered how other relationships flourished from afar.

"You have to move back home so I can stop spending so much time reading your blog updates," wrote my best friend, Paul, from his home in Vermont. "I spend more time interacting with you now than when you lived four hours away."

In the meantime, we were busy developing new relationships in Cambodia which, in many ways, was so much easier.

TALES FROM THE ROAD:
MY LINGUISTIC FAUX PAS-ES: MAY, 2013

A FEW MONTHS INTO OUR LIVING AND LEARNING EXP-
ERIENCE IN CAMBODIA, FRESH FROM A KHMER LANGUAGE
CLASS AND FULL OF POSITIVE ENERGY, I APPROACHED A
WOMAN HOLDING AN ILL BABY IN THE RUSSIAN MARKET AND
ENGAGED HER IN A CONVERSATION IN KHMER.

"JUST JUMP IN," OUR INSTRUCTOR HAD ENTHUSIASTICALLY
INSTRUCTED US.

SO I DID.

"KNYOM KIT TA KOIN NEAK CHIKUIT," I SAID, SMILING
AT HER AND GESTURING TOWARD THE LISTLESS CHILD,
THINKING I HAD JUST TOLD HER WITH GREAT EMPATHY,
"I THINK YOUR CHILD IS SICK."

SHE GLARED AT ME, AND I REALIZED I HAD SUB-STITUTED THE
WORD FOR CRAZY (CHIKUIT) FOR THE WORD FOR SICK (CHEW).

I SUSPECT SHE FORGAVE ME, BUT IF LOOKS WERE
DAGGERS I WOULD HAVE BEEN IN ICU WITHIN MINUTES.

MY WELL-INTENDED LINGUISTIC EXPLOITS YIELDED ALL
SORTS OF CHALLENGING MOMENTS.

ON A RECENT TRIP TO MONDULKIRI WITH MY FRIEND
SARATH TO BOND WITH THE OWNER OF THE GUESTHOUSE

Sarath planned to manage, we were eating dinner with the owner and his wife, who doubles as cook for the place.

The server placed the food on the table, and i decided to engage the owner's wife in some complimentary banter.

"mmmmm mahope nih sa-ooey," i said, smiling, also realizing in horror that i had substituted the word for yummy (chingoey) with the word for stinky (sa-ooey.) i corrected myself, but not before the damage was done.

She was kind to me, but i don't think i'll be on her party invitation list in the future.

My errors are always innocent but severe.

Friends Heang and Konthea pointed out that i had mispronounced the word "Ai Ka Dum" (excellency) at a dinner Gabi and i attended with a bunch of wealthy business owners. i had addressed them as "Ai Ka Dom." Though the difference to my ear was subtle, i had called these esteemed leaders "pieces of excrement."

Maybe that's why we weren't invited to take part in the endless rounds of toasts that's a staple at the big shots' tables?

I've committed any number of linguistic sins. In Cambodia, a slight change of sound often means disaster. Western brains struggle with the weird combinations of sounds. Western tongues turn the simplest of phrases into searing insults.

To make matters worse, Cambodians have a hard time cutting a well-intended baraing (foreigner) any slack. You can wave your arm straight forward like an NFL referee signaling a first down and tell a tuk-tuk driver, "tow trong, tow trong" (go straight, go straight) but they'll baat sdam (turn right) or chwain (left) if they don't get what you're saying. Three years into this experience, I still could not order a coffee with milk

"Cafe duk da kho teuk gaw" without inspiring a furrowed brow and glazed-eyed confusion—and winding up with a black coffee.

The Khmer language is unlike horseshoes and hand grenades: there is no "close enough," only direct hits. "Chew" is sick, but "choo" is sour. "Teuk se-ew" is soy sauce; "teuk sa-ooey" is stinky water (see above.) "Twerr kha" is work; "trow kha" is need. It's important to be precise in your word choice, otherwise you can wind up with a sick soup

MADE OF STINKY WATER, WHICH I SUPPOSE WOULD POSE A CHALLENGE TO STOMACH ("PUA" VS. SNAKE, WHICH IS "PUH.")

I HAVE A FRIEND WHO IS MARRIED TO A KHMER WOMAN; HIS LANGUAGE SKILLS FALL SHORT OF MY OWN. ONE DAY HE DECIDED TO USE THE NATIVE TONGUE WHILE ORDERING HIS DAILY COFFEE FROM HIS REGULAR SHOP. HE PRACTICED IN HIS HEAD AND STEELED HIMSELF FOR THE EXPERIENCE AS HE APPROACHED THE VENDOR, WHO WAS SURROUNDED BY A COLLECTION OF TUK-TUK DRIVERS AND CUSTOMERS STANDING AROUND AND DRINKING COFFEE SWEET ENOUGH TO MELT YOUR BICUSPIDS.

"KNYOM JANG BANH CAFE TOM KMAOW KADOIE." MY FRIEND CRUNCHED THROUGH THE REQUEST, THINKING HE'D JUST ORDERED A LARGE HOT BLACK COFFEE. HE FAILED, HOWEVER, TO ACKNOWLEDGE THAT HE HAD SUBSTITUTED THE WORD FOR HOT "KDAOW" WITH THE WORD FOR PENIS "KDAOIE", WHICH EXPLAINED THE KNEES-ON-HANDS OUTBURST OF LAUGHTER FROM EVERYONE WITHIN EARSHOT.

COFFEE TIME HAD NEVER BEEN SO MUCH FUN FOR THE LOCALS, WHO REPEATED THE ERRANT PHRASE TIME AND AGAIN, EACH COURSE PROMPTING A NEW ROUND

OF SCREECHING LAUGHTER. I'M NOT SURE MY FRIEND LEFT THE STAND WITH ANYTHING MORE THAN WOUNDED PRIDE AND A NOTE TO HIMSELF TO SPEAK ENGLISH IN THE FUTURE.

TO DO ANYTHING ELSE WOULD BE "CHIKUIT."

7
Adapting to Change

I *stepped from the cool shower into the searing early morning heat of Phnom Penh, toweled dry and sat down on the edge of our bed directly in front of the fan. Within seconds it was difficult to tell the difference between the shower's residue and beads of sweat.*

I dressed quickly, instantly soaking through my short-sleeved shirt, and followed Gabi down the two flights of stairs from our apartment into Som On's waiting tuk-tuk to head to work.

Moments later I walked into the air-conditioned comfort of my shared office at Cambodians for Resource Revenue Transparency (CRRT). My friend and boss, Chhay Sarath, looked up and assessed me from across the room.

"Oh, you look fat and sweaty today!" he exclaimed, in the inimitably frank style of a Cambodian commenting on the specter of a slightly paunchy middle-aged foreigner showing the effects of Phnom Penh's relentless heat.

This was life in "the Penh" as we called it, constant exposure to the brain-to-mouth blurting of a culture that paid no heed to personal space, sensitivities or sensibilities.

"Thanks for the compliment," I laughed, easing into my chair. "I love you, too." He scowled, baffled as usual by my sarcastic sense of humor, which simply doesn't resonate in most Cambodian minds.

Getting used to a culture where "no" often means the opposite, where deferring to older, richer and more powerful provides social order, and where "saving face" is about preserving a sense of self forced us to shelve preconceptions, rethink our priorities, and create vast reservoirs of patience.

Our volunteer positions proved worthwhile yet frustrating since we were still getting used to working within a different culture. While we developed deep personal relationships with Cambodian staff, we vented endlessly to each other about our role in the continuum of reports-to-justify-donors' money that seemed to drive the Phnom Penh economy.

Gabi had a healthier relationship with her workplace than I, as she was providing English support to create the mountains of reports most NGOs churn out, and training to those open to learning new skills. I grew increasingly frustrated by the infighting and dispiriting commitment to process that consumed the organization I was working for, a coalition of NGOs trying to find a way to lobby the immovable government on oil, gas and mining policy.

My suggestions for consensus building fell on deaf ears. My recommendation to change the charter of Cambodians for Resource Revenue Transparency (CRRT) to empower them to engage in direct advocacy was ignored in lieu of the status quo of endless meetings and pointless initiatives.

My idealism shattered, I grew restless and increasingly unhappy. I had come to Cambodia thinking I could have an impact on the landscape. "I know politics," I had thought. "I understand business. I can help change things." Six months into the experience, I realized that I was imposing my standards, style and work nature on a group of people who truly cared but were incapable of running at such a pace. They followed a different set of rules adapted to centuries of embedded social conduct.

I should have known better.

We had been told that we'd need to adapt to this culture instead of convincing the culture to adapt to us. I shelved my goals at work, and started to focus on specific people I cared about in the office.

I set new goals that not only helped my colleagues but also helped me regain my sense of value. Those goals focused on two people who quickly became close friends: Heang Thy, our communications officer, and Sarath Chhay, my boss. Heang was keen to find a new job and needed to obtain foreign work experience to discover a new direction; Sarath wanted to find more fulfilling work that was better suited to his personality and skills.

In the time we'd worked together, Heang had become almost like an adopted daughter. She shared her frustrations and personal problems with me, which was an unusual gift of no-strings-attached trust for a younger Khmer woman to bestow on a foreigner. I saw in her something special; she's a Cambodian woman whose wiring has for some reason been altered, allowing her to have a more linear relationship with effort, process and outcome than the majority of her countrymen and women. People like Heang represent the future of Cambodia, in my opinion: educated, honest, fair, open and capable of change.

Heang yearned to leave CRRT, longing for exposure to the U.S. and aspiring to run her own company. She had earned a master's degree in communications from Hong Kong Baptist University and had taken full advantage of the opportunity her advanced education made possible. She needed a mentor. I willingly accepted.

Drawing on my experience as a guest advisor in Ukraine through the International Research and Exchanges program, I helped Heang successfully apply for an internship in the U.S.

She spent three months in Nevada, working with a local advocacy organization monitoring mining activities in the state.

Heang came back to Cambodia a changed woman. In the U.S. she had seen the effects of open advocacy supported by comprehensive federal regulations that had the support of a judiciary designed to enforce the laws. She saw what real advocacy was, recognized what was lacking in Cambodia and knew the potential of what could be.

Mostly, she found a stronger voice. She has moved through two different positions and is now working for an organization based in Bangkok. She is a different person—still beautiful, kind and friendly, but now extremely poised, confident and more outspoken than ever. On some level, her success is my success. Her promotions warm my heart; I know the role I played in her life. Heang helped show me that I do not always have to adapt to change. I can enact change on a small level through my own culture.

Sarath was a different story. A wonderful, kind-hearted man with a lovely wife and two sons, he was miscast as head of an advocacy NGO. Sarath was a people pleaser, not a fire starter, and as the head of a coalition, he was in the uncomfortable position of serving many masters. It was tearing him apart.

He quickly became my best friend in Cambodia.

We developed a habit of having coffee together most mornings. He taught me nuances of Khmer language and culture and shared insights on life in Cambodia—politics, religion, western influence, the future of the country. I supported and encouraged him, challenged him when he needed it and answered his endless questions about his options for the future and the best way to proceed while caring for his wife and sons and two elderly parents, both of whom have health problems.

Over the course of a year, Sarath and I worked on a plan for him to make a larger life change than the one I had made. He and his brother had tried and failed to create a successful rice farming business on 30-plus hectares (roughly 75 acres) of land in Battambang, Cambodia's second largest city. He applied for numerous scholarships in Australia and Europe in an effort to strengthen his résumé. He worked as general manager of a guesthouse in a northern province of Cambodia and has since worked in the tourism industry.

Sarath faced each of his challenges with the classic Khmer attributes of hard work and acceptance of one's preordained future. "I have to try hard," he would say with a smile. "Of course. It is Cambodian way."

Sarath taught me more about adapting to change than any textbook or seminar. I learned the importance of going slowly, working hard and accepting challenges along the way. He is now working in the tourism industry pursuing new opportunities that appeal to him.

Thinking back to the early days of our time in Cambodia—when I had it in mind to help change the political landscape and make positive development a reality for all Cambodians—it is humbling to note how dramatically circumstances forced me to rethink my goals and objectives.

VIA had warned us all about setting unrealistic goals. They foretold our lives as learners, not teachers, but I hadn't listened.

The student cannot learn—even from the best of teachers—until the student is truly ready.

Work wasn't our only source of anxiety as we settled into new lives in Phnom Penh and figured out how to adapt to new challenges that came our way.

Power cuts, incomprehensibly powerful storms during the rainy season that flooded the streets with a foot of filthy water, and a series of illnesses that followed me throughout the threeplus years we lived there all challenged our ability to roll with the punches.

But the arrival of Mr. Rat turned us upside down more than any other event.

My visiting daughter Kirsty was the first to spy the reclusive rodent one night as he scampered along the floorboard from her bedroom to the open door leading to the balcony. She informed me of his presence the next morning. I was ready for battle when he reappeared that night.

I spotted the little bugger running across the floor and instantly gave chase. He headed up the curtains. I swatted at him with a broom. He bolted for our bedroom, causing Gabi to beat a hasty retreat to our bathroom where she barricaded herself behind a locked door. Kirsty, alerted to the fuss, leapt onto our bed as I chased the rat around the room with a broom in one hand and a mop in another.

It was a Keystone Kops escapade of the most ridiculous order, Mr. Rat having the upper hand throughout. Half an hour later, he scampered along a power line leading to our balcony, wounded and winded, but alive. In the days to come I caught several more in the traps I bought at the local market. I like to think Mr. Rat was one of them.

Rat infestations—along with gastrointestinal disorders—are common problems that bind people together in Phnom Penh. Several weeks after our bedroom incident, I bumped into a friend who owned a local restaurant while we were shopping for a metal rat trap in Psar Orussey. His Cambodian wife did her best to help me find my quarry, but I left without my weapon in tow. A few nights later, we stopped into his restaurant along the river to enjoy one of his delicious pizzas. He beamed when he saw us enter and headed my way with a plastic bag, providing yet another in a long list of firsts. He greeted us with a brand new metal rat trap, then took our order for dinner. Such are the norms of life in Phnom Penh–a city where anything can happen, anytime. Maybe that's why it's branded The Kingdom of Wonder, which I've amended to The Kingdom of I Wonder. Rats and cultural misunderstandings apart, the issue that caused me the most discomfort was a major reason why we eventually decided to leave Cambodia: how the ruling party (Cambodian People's Party) dealt with civil unrest as the CPP stole yet another fraudulent election.

Some of our Cambodian friends were involved in the protests and since none of them suffered injury or worse, they were among the fortunate. Several people were killed and scores were injured in violent clashes between opposition forces and government security, police and military. Conflicts between the harsh Cambodian government and its people are frequent, and while we were, for the most part, exempt from the fallout, from time to time we found ourselves involved.

While out on a bike ride one day I found myself amid hundreds of men and women protesting a land grab that had forced them from their homes.

Having a decent grasp of the language, I chatted with the protesters who sat smiling in the mid-day sun, steps away from rows of police carrying riot shields and clubs. They spoke of the hopeless nature of their plight, and of the uncaring government that was more interested in suppressing their voices than listening to their concerns.

As the election came and went and as the international community objected to widespread election manipulation (there were reports of truckloads of Vietnamese delivered to the polls to vote in favor of the status quo, and of thousands of Cambodians whose names were inexplicably struck from the voting rolls), the mean spiritedness of the government and mistreatment of people we cared deeply about began to weigh heavily upon me. I've been politically active my entire adult life; it's not in my nature to sit idly by while injustice and unfairness is allowed to rule. My choice became clear: get involved, or get out. While we'd been able to adapt to most situations that came our way and were eager to help where we could, this one was a biggie. Over the years, we'd put a lot of effort into finding outlets where we could lend a hand (such as helping Heang and Sarath). We'd also learned when it was sensible to quit and what we should keep our noses out of.

But the political problems of Cambodia were not my fight. I decided to keep my mouth shut and limit my actions, but the looming presence of a corrupt and uncaring government colored our prospects for a future in Cambodia.

TALES FROM THE ROAD:
JUST KILL THEM BOTH: MAY, 2012

"JUST KILL THEM BOTH," SAID THE CAMBODIAN MILITARY
POLICE OFFICER.

THOSE WORDS, TRANSLATED BY PHORN BOPHA, FOREVER
CHANGED LIFE FOR HER COLLEAGUE OLESIA PLOKHII, OUR
27-YEAR-OLD JOURNALIST FRIEND.

OLESIA AND BOPHA HAD BEEN WORKING ON A STORY,
TOURING ILLEGAL LOGGING SITES IN SOUTHERN CAMBODIA
WITH CHUT WUTTY, A 40-YEAR-OLD ENVIRONMENTAL
ACTIVIST WITH A LONG HISTORY OF NOSING INTO THE
BUSINESS OF POWERFUL, RUTHLESS PEOPLE. THIS WAS THE
END THE TRIP, THE LAST STOP ON A TWO-DAY TOUR, AND
THE TENSION WAS HIGH.

AS THEY PULLED INTO THE SITE, WUTTY TOLD THEM TO
TAKE THEIR PHOTOGRAPHS AND CONDUCT THEIR INTERVIEWS
QUICKLY. "IN AND OUT FAST," HE TOLD THEM.

TENSION ESCALATED WHEN FOUR MILITARY POLICE
SHOWED UP ON TWO MOTORBIKES, WITH AK47 ASSAULT
RIFLES STRAPPED ACROSS THEIR BACKS. WORDS WERE
EXCHANGED AND THE ARGUMENT BECAME HEATED.
MOMENTS LATER, WUTTY WAS DEAD, SLUMPED IN HIS LATE-

MODEL FOUR-WHEEL DRIVE. A MILITARY OFFICER LAY DEAD
ON THE GROUND NEARBY.

NEITHER JOURNALIST SAW WHO SHOT WHOM. OLESIA WAS
AT THE FRONT OF THE VEHICLE HELPING JUMPSTART THE
CAR, WHICH HAD FALTERED IN AN ODD TWIST OF BAD TIMING
WITH SEVERE CONSEQUENCES. BOPHA, TOO, WAS OUT OF
THE LINE OF SIGHT AND DID NOT SEE WHO FIRED THE
SHOTS.

THE OFFICIAL REPORT: "MILITARY POLICE OFFICER
IN RATANA SHOT AND KILLED. WUTTY THEN TURNED
HIS AK47 ON HIMSELF, SHOOTING HIMSELF NOT ONCE
BUT TWICE, AND DYING INSTANTLY." THE IMPLAUSIBILITY
OF THE MURDER/SUICIDE ECHOED AROUND CAMBODIA
AMID CRIES FOR AN INDEPENDENT INVESTIGATION. IN A
COUNTRY OF CAREFULLY WOVEN SCRIPTS AND STRIDENT
OFFICIAL DECLARATIONS, THE WORDS "INDEPENDENT" AND
"INVESTIGATION" ARE BUT ABSTRACT NOTIONS.

WHAT HAPPENED TO OLESIA AND BOPHA ROBBED THEM
OF WHAT WAS LEFT OF THEIR INNOCENCE AND DENIED
THEM THEIR RIGHTS AND PROTECTIONS AS JOURNALISTS.
THEY WERE DETAINED AT THE SIGHT OF THE SHOOTINGS
FOR AN HOUR AND A HALF WHILE THE MILITARY POLICE
DEBATED THEIR NEXT MOVE.

EVENTUALLY FREED, THEY WERE RELEASED INTO THEIR
RESPECTIVE HELLS OF FEAR, CONFUSION AND MISGUIDED

ADVICE, ADDING THE BITTER TASTE OF UNCERTAINTY TO AN ALREADY ACIDIC RECIPE FOR DANGER AND DISASTER.

THEY WILL NEVER KNOW WHAT CAUSED THE OFFICERS TO SPARE THEM. THAT THEY WERE JOURNALISTS? THAT ONE OF THEM WAS A FOREIGNER (OLESIA IS CANADIAN)? THAT THEY WERE WOMEN?

WE OFFERED OLESIA REFUGE IN OUR HOME. OVER THE NEXT THREE DAYS AS WE HUDDLED TOGETHER AND ACCOMPANIED HER TO MEETINGS WITH VARIOUS AUTHORITIES, WE SAW HER WILL, INTEGRITY AND INTELLIGENCE TESTED AND REAFFIRMED AS VARIOUS ORGANIZATIONS AND INDIVIDUALS BOMBARDED HER WITH CONFLICTING ADVICE:

GO. STAY. TALK.

BE SILENT.

TALK TO THE MEDIA.

YOU MAY NOT TALK TO THE MEDIA (THIS FROM HER EMPLOYER, THE CAMBODIAN DAILY, OF ALL IRONIES).

YOU HAVE NO DUTY TO ANYONE AND SHOULD FLEE THE COUNTRY TO PROTECT YOURSELF.

YOU HAVE A RESPONSIBILITY TO STAY HERE, OFFER SUPPORT AND (OSTENSIBLY) INDIRECT PROTECTION FOR YOUR CAMBODIAN COUNTERPART, WHO IS AT EVEN GREATER RISK.

DO NOT GO OUT AT NIGHT.

DO NOT BE ALONE. EVER.

DO NOT RIDE A MOTORBIKE, AS THAT'S WHERE MANY "ACCIDENTS" HAPPEN TO PEOPLE TARGETED FOR REMOVAL BY POWERFUL GHOSTS . TUK-TUKS ARE ONLY MARGINALLY BETTER; CARS THE MOST SECURE. ONE ORGANIZATION OFFERED TO MAKE A CAR AND DRIVER AVAILABLE 24 HOURS, AND TO PLACE HER IN A SAFE HOUSE.

IMAGINE BEING A TRAUMATIZED YOUNG REPORTER PRESENT DURING TWO SHOOTING DEATHS WHOSE LIFE HAS BEEN THREATENED BY MEN WITH GUNS.

IMAGINE THE EFFECTS OF FATIGUE, STRESS, AND MEMORIES OF TWO MEN LYING DEAD-ONE OF WHOM YOU HAD COME TO KNOW WELL, ADMIRE AND CARE ABOUT-AND SOMEHOW FINDING A CLEAR HEAD TO WEIGH YOUR OPTIONS.

IMAGINE BELIEVING SOMETHING EVIL COULD HAPPEN TO YOU AT ANY MOMENT.

IMAGINE THE VULNERABILITY, MADE WORSE BY AN AVALANCHE OF CONFLICTING INFORMATION INTENDED TO HELP.

YOU AND YOUR FRIENDS ARE BEING MONITORED. EMAILS, PHONE CALLS, TEXTS. MAKE ONLY SKYPE CALLS; SKYPE DOCUMENT TRANSFER AND FAXES ARE REASONABLY SAFE FOR CONFIDENTIAL COMMUNICATION.

THE GOVERNMENT-THE FORCES BEHIND THE PEOPLE WHO PUT YOUR LIFE IN DANGER AND KILLED YOUR FRIEND-KNOW YOUR WHEREABOUTS AT ALL TIMES.

IMAGINE A YOUNG WOMAN WHO FACES ALL THESE BITS OF ADVICE, THE "WISDOM," THE COUNSEL, THE SUGGESTIONS AND EVEN THE INSTRUCTIONS-WHO SOMEHOW FINDS THE COURAGE, INTELLIGENCE AND STRENGTH TO MAKE INFORMED, SMART DECISIONS.

HER DECISION INVOLVED MUCH MORE THAN JUST STAYING OR GOING. LEAVING WOULD DESTROY HER SOUL; STAYING COULD END HER LIFE.

SHE CHOSE OUR HOME AS REFUGE AS SHE CONFRONTED THESE COMPLEX QUESTIONS WITH DIRE CONSEQUENCES, AND I AM FOREVER GRATEFUL THAT SHE DID.

I WILL ALWAYS BE IN AWE OF HOW STRONG OLESIA WAS THROUGHOUT HER ORDEAL, OF HOW SHE SAW THE FACTS OF THE SITUATION WHILE FEELING THE EMOTIONS OF IT ALL, YET SOMEHOW FOUND A WAY TO KEEP SOLID BARRIERS BETWEEN FACT AND SPECULATION, EMOTION AND ANALYSIS.

IN THE END, SHE MADE THE SMART DECISION. SHE CHOSE TO LEAVE.

SHE LEFT THE COUNTRY, BUT NOT THE ISSUES THAT CAUSED HER TO FACE DANGER AND DEATH. SHE DIDN'T LEAVE THE STORY OF THE MAN WHO ACCEPTED RISK AS AN OCCUPATIONAL HAZARD AND WAS AWARE THAT DEATH WAS A POSSIBILITY EVERY DAY. SHE LEFT THE COUNTRY PHYSICALLY, BUT DID NOT ABANDON HER ROLE IN THE

CRAZY, CONTRASTED WORLD OF CAMBODIA—"A COUNTRY WHERE HEROES DIE," ONE COMMENTED.

I PICKED HER UP AFTER A LATE-AFTERNOON APPOINTMENT, TOLD HER I'D BOOKED HER FLIGHT AND THAT SHE WAS LEAVING IN 45 MINUTES. WE TOOK HER BACK TO OUR PLACE, WHERE SHE PACKED A SMALL BAG, SORTED OUT HER PASSPORT AND MONEY AND BRAVELY STEPPED INTO THE TUK-TUK FOR THE 30-MINUTE RIDE TO THE AIRPORT.

AFTER DEPOSITING HER AT THE DEPARTURE GATE AND IMMERSING HER IN HUGS AND TEARS, WE DROVE ACROSS THE STREET, SAT IN A SMALL RESTAURANT, SIPPED BEER AND WAITED FOR THE PREARRANGED CODED MESSAGE THAT WOULD LET US KNOW SHE HAD MADE IT THROUGH SECURITY AND WAS ON THE PLANE SAFELY EN ROUTE TO BANGKOK.

MY PHONE BEEPED. "ON."

AND WITH THAT, SHE WAS GONE. AND SHE WAS SAFE.

8
Healthcare

I *opened the door to the International SOS Clinic on Street 51*
in central Phnom Penh. With paper bag in hand, I approached
the receptionist. "I have an appointment," I said, giving her my
name and telephone number. "What's the problem?" asked the young
Cambodian woman in perfect English. "Stomach upset, gastrointes-
tinal problems," I muttered. "We'll need a stool sample..." she began,
stopping when I raised the paper bag to her eye level. A veteran of
Cambodian gastrointestinal wars, I had come prepared.

My mind drifted back three years earlier, during a tour of SOS
with the nurse manager as part of our "welcome to Phnom Penh"
offerings through Volunteers in Asia. We strolled the air-conditioned
corridors past treatment rooms and a triage center, then settled into
a conference room for an overview and question and answer period.
"Most health problems here are minor," she said. "You can avoid most
problems by washing your hands frequently and refusing ice, which

is loaded with nasty bacteria. But this is the tropics, and there are
bugs, bacteria and all sorts of nasties everywhere.
  "Things are going to happen, and if you have any aversion to talking
about poop, get over it."

Taking care of our health and protecting ourselves from scary
and unfamiliar diseases was a top priority when we moved to
Cambodia.

Before we departed, fueled by a well-intended but overly fear-
based session at our 2010 VIA training on recommended immunizations, Gabi and I spent hours online researching the Centers for
Disease Control website and comparing notes from people who'd
lived in the region about how to prepare and protect ourselves.

The list was overwhelming: Japanese encephalitis, hepatitis,
yellow fever, rabies, malaria. On and on went the list of threats,
infections and things we'd best worry about, followed by an
equally long list of recommended shots and pills.

We wound up selecting immunizations for the life-threatening
and prevalent diseases reported in Cambodia (Japanese encephalitis, hepatitis, rabies) and getting boosters of the basics (teta-
nus, etc.) Researching online, we learned the chances of catching some of the more exotic and rare diseases like cholera and
yellow fever were slim.

I've been blessed with good health my entire life, but living in the germ factories of Southeast Asia took me to my knees on many occasions. Gabi, having grown up in the Persian Gulf and having been exposed to life in undeveloped countries, seems immune to just about everything.

I grew accustomed to periodically catching nasty gastro-intestinal infections. I'd lie awake during the night with a familiar rumbling that would erupt as the night progressed. Next morning, I'd be on my way to the International SOS clinic, stool sample in hand, anticipating a prescription of antibiotics and a supply of rehydrating fluids. It became no big deal, except for the inconvenience.

Disease was a way of life in Cambodia. One group of Australian volunteers we were friendly with established a betting pool to see who would be the last to "go down" with a gastro infection as they became acclimated to the microbes that flourish in Phnom Penh. If you can't beat it, have fun with it.

We learned the importance of being resourceful when, inevitably, things happened. VIA did a great job introducing us to the SOS clinic when we first arrived. As time passed, our network of friends in Phnom Penh—as well as the invaluable Yahoo group Cambodian Parents Network—helped us find a physical therapist, a naturopath and even a gifted trigger point massage therapist who helped us address issues when they arose.

I packed a medical kit full of over-the-counter meds and first aid supplies when we traveled to remote areas. I also tossed in a few meds like Ciprofloxacin, which is vital for combating some of the nastier intestinal infections.

Make no mistake about the reality of healthcare in Cambodia: medical care for foreigners is rudimentary for the most part (even though there are examples where people were treated well for injuries and illnesses). Our friend Cori Parks, for example, received excellent treatment when she was knocked from her bicycle in Phnom Penh traffic and rushed to the emergency room. But quality care is a crapshoot, inconsistent and unreliable. Most foreigners opt out, choosing medical evacuation to Bangkok, Singapore or Malaysia when serious problems strike.

Cambodians, however—particularly the masses of poor or low-income families (80% live on less than $2 per day)—are forced to rely on traditional healing methods, substandard care and facilities, and often quackery.

Health insurance was important to us, and our VIA relationship came with a fantastic policy through International Educational Exchange Services (IEES). This New York-based company proved to be the antithetical insurance company— accessible, responsive and customer friendly.

I gave my IEES card a serious workout through countless bouts of "Delhi belly," bronchial infections, two battles with

dengue fever and one with malaria. The local clinic suited us perfectly fine for minor issues, but for anything more serious or involved, or for our annual physicals, we headed to Bumrungrad International Hospital in Bangkok.

The series of afflictions I experienced in Cambodia seemed relatively insignificant, however, when I contracted not one but two strains of malaria while touring India. I awoke in the middle of night shivering uncontrollably in our hotel room in Bikaner and realized something was seriously wrong. We grabbed a train the next day to New Delhi, checked back into the AirBnB where we had stayed when we first arrived in India, and asked our host to help find medical attention.

That led to one of the worst healthcare experiences of my life, prompting us to bolt from the hospital in New Delhi to a nearby Starbucks, where we logged onto our laptops and booked a flight to Bangkok.

Within minutes of showing up at Bumrungrad , I was whisked into the emergency room and put on an intravenous drip while staff consulted with a U.S.-trained tropical disease expert. The genuine concern, gentleness and care I experienced in the next four days raised the bar for healthcare and set a new standard with which I am unwilling to compromise.

Our experiences at Bumrungrad serve as sober reminders about the problems of U.S. healthcare while reminding us how good and affordable healthcare can be. Walking into this hospital is like checking into a five-star hotel, where receptionists clad in soft green silk speak multiple languages and direct patients to world-class specialists who can be seen pretty much on-demand. The place oozes excellence. I've visited my share of hospitals in the U.S. and cannot think of a hospital visit that would compare favorably to what we experienced in Thailand on numerous occasions.

Best of all, high quality medical care costs a fraction of what it does in the West. What's missing at Bumrungrad and other Asian hospitals are the long waits and impenetrable bureaucratic barriers.

Gabi once met with a specialist at Bumrungrad to address an ongoing medical situation. Western trained and an acknowledged leader in his field, he confidently explained her issue as a transient problem and offered full details in an easy-going manner. He quietly answered her questions, made sure she fully understood his diagnosis, then charged her $20.40 for the visit.

I once saw a western-trained orthopedic surgeon in Thailand to seek opinions on my two creaky hips (one of which was replaced roughly 10 years ago). I paid about $150 for two consultations with an experienced specialist and detailed x-rays of both hips.

My four-day stay for malaria treatment cost $2,500, was covered fully by IEES and serves as the ultimate example of how good Thai medical care can be.

As my malaria symptoms eased and I began to feel better, my doctor (Dr. Wichai Techasathit, who had a master's degree in public health from the University of Washington and completed a clinical fellowship in infectious diseases at New England Medical Center in Boston), wrapped up the review of my progress and turned to Gabi.

"How are you?" he asked, exhibiting genuine concern for her health as well as how the stress of dealing with a sick husband had affected her. His attention struck us as well beyond the norm and emphasized the differences between care in the East and West. Once a year we underwent our regular physicals at Bumrungrad—extensive, thorough, half-day-long processes that concluded with a lengthy, unhurried evaluation with our doctors, that included recommendations on diet and exercise to address specific issues. Every experience we had there gave us great access to quality medical personnel who were also kind and easy to talk to.

We discovered the same blend of high quality care and low cost when we discovered Roomchang Dental and Aesthetic Hospital in Phnom Penh. Over two years of visits, Roomchang's director

Dr. Tith Hong Yeou became a friend and colleague. The dental care I received from Dr. Chav Bunhean was second to none, again at a fraction of the cost of a U.S. dental practice. Cleanings were $25, including x-rays. I had two crowns replaced while in Phnom Penh, each costing less than $500. And all the procedures were performed in gleaming, state of the art facilities, by English-speaking, western-trained dentists. Small wonder that Roomchang's dental tourism business is attracting foreigners with its low cost and high quality.

Once our contracts with VIA expired—also ending our IEES health insurance—we signed on with World Nomads. This cost-effective insurance covers us for significant events. Gabi had a fantastic experience with them when securing coverage for treatment of a neck problem that totaled more than $1,000. We spend about $250 per month on coverage for both of us. Most of the people we interviewed for this book are World Nomads clients, too. The balance use other private insurance companies or pay for medical expenses out of pocket.

Many countries, incidentally, offer free medical care to everyone—tourists included. Having sought help in an emergency room in Italy, upon being discharged I elicited a shrug and a scowl from the doctor who treated me when I asked for the bill. "This is Italy," he said. "Health care is a basic human right."

TALES FROM THE ROAD:
WHERE HEALTH CARE MEANS POOR CARE:
APRIL, 2011

THE ROOM WAS 25 BY 10 FEET, CRAMMED WITH FIVE
METAL BEDS COVERED WITH BLUE RUBBER MATTRESSES.

FOUR OF THE BEDS WERE OCCUPIED: ONE BY A
SEMICONSCIOUS OLD MAN WITH AN IV IN HIS ARM, ANOTHER
BY A MIDDLE-AGED MAN WITH HIS PANTS BUNCHED
AROUND HIS ANKLES, A THIRD BY A YOUNG CHILD WHOSE
PLAINTIVE WAILS MOUNTED AS THE DOCTOR APPROACHED
AND THE FOURTH BY MY FRIEND TONY'S WIFE, PAOLLA.

TONY HAD CALLED ME FOR HELP, ABANDONING HIS POST
AS A TUK-TUK DRIVER IN A PANIC. PAOLLA HAD BEEN
SICK FOR MONTHS, FIRST WITH A THYROID CONDITION THAT
REQUIRED SURGERY AND THEN WITH STOMACH AND THROAT
COMPLICATIONS THAT LEFT HER UNABLE TO EAT, SWALLOW
COMFORTABLY OR SLEEP.

WE ARRIVED AT THEIR "ROOM" IN PHNOM PENH THEY
AFTER A 30-MINUTE DASH IN TONY'S TUK-TUK THROUGH
PHNOM PENH'S CHAOTIC STREETS. WE FOUND PAOLLA
CURLED UP ON THEIR SLEEPING MAT IN THE 10X10 FOOT
ROOM THEY CALL HOME. SHE WAS AWAKE BUT LISTLESS
AND IN EXTREME DISCOMFORT.

AFTER TONY CHATTED QUIETLY WITH HER FOR A FEW MOMENTS, WE HELPED HER INTO THE TUK-TUK TO TAKE HER TO THE NEARBY CLINIC. TONY DECLINED MY OFFER TO TAKE HER TO THE SOS INTERNATIONAL CLINIC THAT GABI AND I USE. "TOO EXPENSIVE," HE PROTESTED, IGNORING MY OFFER TO PAY.

SO OFF TO THE LOCAL CLINIC WE WENT, PAOLLA AND ME IN THE BACK OF THE TUK-TUK AND TONY WEAVING THROUGH THE TRAFFIC. PAOLLA REACHED OUT TO ME, PLACING A LEATHERY HAND ATOP MINE, AND SMILED.

"ORKUHN CHRAN," SHE SAID, LOOKING ME DEEPLY IN THE EYES. "THANK YOU VERY MUCH." SHE POINTED OUT THE CLINIC TO TONY, WHO WOULD HAVE SPED PAST HAD SHE NOT INTERVENED. HUSTLING INSIDE, WE WERE DIRECTED TOWARD AN EMPTY BED.

WELCOME TO HEALTH CARE, CAMBODIAN STYLE, REPLETE WITH DIRTY FLOORS, UNSANITARY CONDITIONS (THERE WERE BLOODY GAUZE PADS ON THE FLOOR BENEATH PAOLLA'S BED) AND AN ARRAY OF DOCTORS WITH GRUBBY LAB COATS AND DUBIOUS CREDENTIALS OFFERING QUESTIONABLE DIAGNOSES AND TREATMENTS. THIS IS A COUNTRY THAT SPENDS LESS THAN $3 PER CAPITA PER YEAR ON HEALTH CARE. MORE THAN 75% OF TOTAL HEALTH CARE SPENDING IS FROM PRIVATE-PAY SOURCES, MEANING YOU GET CARE ONLY IF YOU HAVE MONEY. NO ONE TOOK HER VITAL SIGNS.

NO ONE LOOKED AT THE BAG OF PILLS I HAD SUGGESTED
TONY BRING ALONG TO SHOW WHAT PAOLLA HAD BEEN
PREVIOUSLY GIVEN FOR HER AILMENTS.

AFTER SEVERAL CURSORY VISITS BY MEN AND WOMEN IN
LAB COATS, A DOCTOR APPEARED WHO WAS SLIGHTLY OLDER,
SEEMED MORE CREDIBLE, AND THANKFULLY SPOKE FAIRLY
GOOD ENGLISH.

"SHE HAS HIGH BLOOD PRESSURE," HE ANNOUNCED.

140 OVER 102 DOESN'T SEEM THAT HIGH FOR SOMEONE
WHO'S STRESSED, DEHYDRATED AND HASN'T EATEN
ANYTHING BUT RICE PORRIDGE FOR WEEKS, I THOUGHT TO
MYSELF. I TOOK ANOTHER TACK.

"WHAT IS THE CONDITION OF HER THROAT?" I ASKED.
HIPAA LAWS DON'T EXIST IN CAMBODIA, SO DOCS HERE ARE
APPARENTLY FREE TO TALK ABOUT ANYONE'S CONDITION
WITH ANY JERK FROM THE STREET. HE OBLIGED.

"SHE HAS NOTHING WRONG INSIDE HER THROAT. IT IS
FINE, JUST SOME PHARANXITIS (MILD IRRITATION). I AM
GIVING HER MEDICINE FOR THAT, AND FOR HER HIGH
BLOOD PRESSURE, AND SOMETHING TO HELP HER SLEEP."

THIS IS A HARD EDGE OF LIFE IN CAMBODIA FROM WHICH I
AM COMFORTABLY EXEMPT. CAMBODIANS ARE ON THEIR OWN.
AS I WATCHED TONY TENDERLY KNEAD HIS WIFE'S CALVES,
OFFERING CAMBODIAN-STYLE RELIEF THAT IS THEIR
ANSWER TO MOST MALADIES, I FELT THEIR SOLITUDE.

I SAW THE POTENTIAL FOR MISDIAGNOSIS AND ERROR IN CAMBODIA'S ROADSIDE CLINICS. IT IS A CRAPSHOOT, A GUESSING GAME WITH A LIFE AT STAKE. AND THOUGH IT'S NOT FAIR TO ASSUME CAMBODIAN DOCTORS' INTEREST IN PROVIDING CARE IS AS WOEFUL AS THEIR FORMAL TRAINING, I WOULDN'T TAKE A PET TO ONE OF THESE CLINICS.

AFTER ABOUT 30 MINUTES TONY INFORMED ME HIS SISTER WAS ON THE WAY TO STAY WITH PAOLLA. WE GOT READY TO LEAVE. THE DOCTOR APPEARED AGAIN WITH A FISTFUL OF PILLS, CRYPTIC INSTRUCTIONS IN KHMER, AND QUICK BUT KINDLY ANSWERS TO MY QUESTIONS ABOUT WHAT PAOLLA SHOULD BE EATING TO REGAIN HER STRENGTH.

WE HELPED PAOLLA OUT THE DOOR, BACK INTO THE TUK-TUK AND GOT ON OUR WAY TO THEIR ROOM, WHERE SHE ONCE AGAIN CURLED UP WITH A FRESH LOAD OF PILLS NEXT TO HER. TONY AND I WERE OFF: HE TO SEEK A TUK-TUK FARE ON THE STREETS OF PHNOM PENH TO PAY FOR THE TREATMENT AND MEDICATION; ME, TO DISAPPEAR BACK INTO AN ENTITLED LIFE THAT HAD NO RELEVANCE TO SUCH PROBLEMS.

PAOLLA RETURNED TO THE ISOLATION OF A HOT ROOM, ILLS THAT WON'T GO AWAY, AND PILLS THAT DID NOTHING TO EASE HER PAIN.

TALES FROM THE ROAD:
MALARIA MADNESS ... FEVERS, CHILLS
AND THE COOKIE DOCTOR: SEPTEMBER, 2013

IN MY ALTERED STATE OF MALARIA-INDUCED FOGGINESS,
NEW DELHI'S INDIRA GANDHI AIRPORT PRESENTED ITSELF
AS A TWISTED MASS OF CONCRETE AND STEEL.

STEPPING FROM THE CAR TO THE CURB, I FELT THE WORLD
SPIRAL. A MONSOON CLOUDBURST OF NAUSEA WASHED OVER
ME. BATHED IN SWEAT AND WITH MY HEAD SPINNING, I
CROUCHED AND WRAPPED MY ARMS AROUND A NEARBY
POLE FOR SUPPORT, DREW SHORT, SHALLOW BREATHS, AND
STARED AT THE SIDEWALK.

"HONEY, LOOK INTO MY EYES," SAID A VOICE NEXT TO ME.
OH, IT'S GABI. WHY AM I LOOKING UP AT HER? AND WHO IS
SPLASHING WATER ON ME? WHO'S SLAPPING MY FACE?

SOMEONE HELPED ME SIT UP AND PROPPED ME AGAINST
A STEEL FENCE, WRESTLING OFF MY BACKPACK. A GROUP
HAD GATHERED. ONE MAN HANDED ME A BOTTLE OF
WATER. I SIPPED IT, GRINNED AND TOLD THEM I WAS FINE.

I HAD PASSED OUT, CLAIMED BY FATIGUE, DIZZINESS AND
DEHYDRATION BROUGHT ON BY WHAT LATER WOULD BE
DIAGNOSED AS A DOUBLE DOSE OF MALARIA. TWO AIRPORT

DOCTORS APPEARED, TOOK MY VITAL SIGNS AND ASKED ME MEDICAL HISTORY QUESTIONS. A WHEELCHAIR APPEARED, AND AFTER RECEIVING CLEARANCE FROM THE DOCTORS, GABI AND I WERE FAST-TRACKED PAST THE LINES OF PEOPLE AND INTO THE TERMINAL.

"WAIT," SAID THE PORTER PUSHING THE WHEELCHAIR. "THE MAN WHO GAVE YOU THE WATER. HE WANTS 10 RUPEES FOR IT." TYPICAL OF INDIA: KINDNESS AND COMPASSION ARE FREE, BUT WATER COSTS MONEY, IN THIS CASE ABOUT 15 CENTS.

THIS ODYSSEY HAD BEGUN TWO DAYS EARLIER, WHEN GABI AND I WERE IN BIKANER, RAJASTHAN WHERE A ROUND OF CHILLS AND SHIVERS HIT ME WITHOUT WARNING— MY OWN PERSONAL EARTHQUAKE, A TEETH-RATTLING, MUSCLE-TWITCHING SHAKEDOWN THAT SEEMED TO GO ON FOREVER. EACH ROUND WAS FOLLOWED BY A SWEAT BATH WORTHY OF A WRESTLER TRYING TO MAKE WEIGHT. A PULSATING HEADACHE SETTLED IN, JOINED BY A PERSISTENT BACKACHE THAT FELT LIKE I'D BEEN BRUTALLY KIDNEY PUNCHED.

THE FOLLOWING MORNING, WE FACED A NINE-HOUR TRAIN RIDE TO NEW DELHI PRECEDED BY A BUMPY 45-MINUTE AUTO RICKSHAW RIDE TO THE STATION AND THE TYPICAL CHAOS ONE ENCOUNTERS IN AN INDIAN TRAIN STATION.

I CLIMBED INTO MY TOP BERTH, WRAPPED MYSELF IN THE WORN BUT CLEAN SHEETS, AND DISAPPEARED INTO

A PROLONGED DAZE, I SWEATED, SHIVERED AND EASED IN AND OUT OF SLEEP FOR THE NEXT EIGHT HOURS, MISERABLE, HOT AND COLD AT THE SAME TIME, UNTIL WE PASSED INTO THE NEW DELHI TRAIN TERMINAL THROUGH THE VAST SLUM AROUND THE TRAIN STATION.

MY STRATEGY WAS TO GET TO A HOSPITAL IN NEW DELHI THE NEXT MORNING. OUR AIRBNB HOSTS, PUSHP AND VINITA, TOOK US TO THE HOSPITAL AND RELUCTANTLY LEFT US THERE. "DON'T LET THEM ADMIT YOU," PUSHP WARNED AND LEFT.

A PORTLY DOCTOR IN A STAINED SHORT-SLEEVED SHIRT SAT BEHIND A RUSTY STEEL DESK, HIS OPEN BRIEFCASE BURSTING WITH PAPERS, A MOBILE PHONE AND SEVERAL HALF-EATEN PACKAGES OF COOKIES. IGNORING ME, HE SHUFFLED SOME PAPERS AND MUMBLED UNINTELLIGIBLY.

"WITH YOUR PERMISSION," HE SAID, GRABBING HIS PHONE IN HIS PUDGY FINGERS, "I MUST MAKE AN URGENT PHONE CALL." FOR THE NEXT FEW MINUTES HE PROCEEDED TO SPEAK IN CRYPTIC ENGLISH TO SOME BUREAUCRAT, MAKING SURE HIS APPLICATION TO RECEIVE AN AWARD OF EXCELLENCE HAD ARRIVED ON TIME.

ARE YOU KIDDING ME? PROMOTING YOURSELF IS URGENT BUSINESS?

HIS "URGENT" BUSINESS FINISHED, DR. DON'T CARE PROCEEDED TO TRANSPOSE MY COMPUTER-PRINTED PERSONAL INFORMATION ON THE BACK OF THE FORM I'D

PRESENTED, CAREFULLY WRITING AND SPEAKING ALOUD THE
DETAILS IN A DUPLICATIVE PROCESS THAT BEGAN TO GNAW
AT MY PATIENCE AS MINUTES TICKED BY.

HE INQUIRED ABOUT MY MEDICAL HISTORY THEN GOT
AROUND TO MY SYMPTOMS. HE SCRIBBLED AS I SPOKE, AND
I REALIZED HE WAS WRITING A LIST OF PRESCRIPTIONS
BEFORE EVEN TAKING MY PULSE. ANTIBIOTICS, ANTI-NAUSEA
MEDICATION, TYLENOL!

"I THINK YOU SHOULD BE ADMITTED TO THE HOSPITAL," HE
PRONOUNCED AS PUSHP HAD PREDICTED. I WAVED HIM OFF.
HE SHRUGGED AND CONTINUED TO WRITE AND MUMBLE.

"PATIENT MUST TAKE TEMPERATURE EVERY SIX HOURS
AND WRITE ON PIECE OF PAPER."

HE THEN WAVED ME TO AN EXAMINATION TABLE
COVERED WITH CRUMPLED, USED EXAM-TABLE PAPER, AND
DISPENSED WITH THE FORMALITY OF WASHING HIS HANDS.
HE LISTENED TO MY HEARTBEAT, ROUGHLY SHOVING MY
CHIN NORTHWARD WHEN I TWICE TURNED MY HEAD TO THE
SIDE. HE PROBED MY CHEST AND ABDOMEN AND ASKED IF I
HAD A HEADACHE.

"HORRIBLE," I SAID AS I LAY BEFORE HIM, LOOKING UP. "I
FEEL AS IF MY HEAD'S GOING TO EXPLODE."

WITHOUT WARNING, HE GRABBED MY NOGGIN ON EITHER
SIDE AND BOUNCED THE BACK OF IT ON THE EXAM TABLE

as if testing a melon for ripeness. Too shocked to object or stop him, i was further distressed when he did it again.

i sprang from the table and raced to the safety of the chair, putting the desk between us—a rusted moat of protection from a chubby doctor with sugar crystals on his fingers.

He wrote orders for a blood test, but i'd seen enough of the Max Super Specialty Hospital (i'm not making up this name). Within minutes Gabi and i were out the door, 1,100 rupees (about $19) lighter but with my head and dignity intact.

Within an hour i'd booked flights to Bangkok to the safety of Bumrungrad International Hospital.

The episode at the airport the following day was awful and the flight was horrible, but it was all worthwhile. On Monday, i fell into the care of Bumrungrad's emergency room staff. They took my vitals, confirmed my suspicions of malaria, took blood samples to confirm it, and admitted me without bouncing my head on the exam table and with nary a cookie in sight.

9

Money Matters

*W*hat do you think we'd do if we ran out of money?" I've asked
Gabi on more than one occasion.

*Typically, she looks me as if I'd grown wings or shaved my head,
furrowing her brows: "We'd figure it out."*

*"No, seriously, what would we do? Get jobs? Where would we
live?" "Of course we'd get jobs, and we'd probably live someplace
that's cheap. Like Cambodia."*

*"Huh. I'd always thought that if something happened and we were
broke, we'd head back to the U.S., rent a cheap apartment and try
to get back into the workforce."*

*"Really? Well, that sounds horrible to me," was her answer. And
I agreed.*

*I realize that, at this point, we're damaged—perhaps beyond re-
pair—as far as working in the U.S. again is concerned. We've been
spoiled by the simple, cheap life in Cambodia and I never again
want to wear a tie or put together a PowerPoint presentation*

As we set up our new lives in Cambodia, we became centered around the typical elements of life: where to go and what to see; what to do with friends, and when; how to survive the heat while maintaining an exercise regimen; keeping our sense of humor; and what to do to keep ourselves interested, stimulated and productive.

This stuff all costs money. It would be wise, we concluded, to find some sort of gainful employment to supplement our meager volunteer stipends while lessening the draw on our savings.

As previously mentioned, several opportunities came our way. Gabi began writing for Cambodian magazines and online publications and was hired by an international NGO to write a book about traditional Cambodian desserts. Not long after that, a friend tipped her off that a publishing group was looking for someone to write a chapter about moving to Cambodia for a book on relocating to Southeast Asia. In short order she turned around enough copy to warrant its own book, leading the publisher to release her *Definitive Guide to Moving to Southeast Asia: Cambodia* in 2012.

While neither of these publishing contracts was terribly lucrative, they provided her with opportunities to learn, write and create while earning a few bucks to supplement our income.

A couple hundred dollars is a month's food budget in Cambodia. As my work with CRRT went from full-time to part-time and eventually to an on-call consulting basis, I fell into a routine that, while thoroughly relaxing, was a bit boring: breakfast at home, off to a coffee shop to write, out for a bike ride or a trip to the local casino to try my luck at slots and take advantage of the great air-conditioning and free bottled water. After lunch, a nice nap, then the gym with Gabi, dinner, and some chill time together.

This wasn't going to work for me long-term so I started nosing around for something else to do.

I landed a consulting job to write website copy for a PR/marketing firm owned by a Cambodian-American man I'd met through my work at CRRT. That turned into a business development consulting job for the agency, which also referred me to a local dental practice looking for someone to write copy for their redesigned website.

That short-term job turned into more than two years of enjoyable and rewarding work for Roomchang Dental and Aesthetic Hospital and its director, Dr. Tith Hong Yeou. As the writing gig concluded and Dr. Tith asked me to help him re-think his business strategy and organizational dynamics, something occurred to me: Here I was, a middle-aged guy, an expensive commodity in the U.S. and part of a generation that had become threatened by the retracting U.S. economy. Many people my age had simply given up on working, the situation was so dire. But in Cambodia, talented business owners were more than happy to hire a guy with years of experience—and they were happy to pay top dollar for it.

Over the next two years, through word of mouth, I stumbled from one consulting job to another, providing guidance, advice and support in marketing and public relations strategies, business development, and organization and management. My work with Dr. Tith expanded into a job for both me and Gabi as we helped create a framework to develop the hospital's dental tourism practice and recruit and hire a full time marketing director.

In between stints at Roomchang, I completed a lengthy consulting contract with Sciaroni & Associates, one of Phnom Penh's top law firms, owned by former Reagan White House Counsel Bretton Sciaroni. I knew nothing of law, but I knew a fair piece about marketing and business development—the firm's weak spots. It was a fun and lucrative engagement.

Word of mouth also landed me at a local NGO that provided training and support for other NGOS. VBNK was trying to get organized and find a way to obtain revenue from sources other than international donors. I was hired to work with marketingand business development staff to create a system to identify and solicit business.

These jobs paid extremely well by Cambodian standards, where $700 a month is considered a decent, livable salary, and where the cost of living made stretching a buck an easy proposition. I made enough from these part-time jobs to not only cover our monthly living expenses, but to pay for our unquenchable thirst for travel and experiences in other Southeast Asian countries.

We both wrote for local online publications (travel, restaurant reviews, personal experiences) that paid poorly but provided a mechanism for constantly expanding our universe and exploring new facets of Cambodia. These jobs came from our natural proclivity for networking; we found ourselves tripping over opportunities all the time.

All told, it was easy to find work to pay our way, give us something to focus on and keep us from having to think about going back to the U.S. to work.

10
Personal Security

*A*t around 9 pm on a sultry Saturday night. Skip and I were strolling back to our apartment after dinner at a local restaurant about six blocks away. He walked a few steps ahead of me as we turned the corner onto our quiet, tree-lined street.

Suddenly, a motorbike skimmed my left arm as it swerved around the corner. I felt a tug on my left shoulder and my bag was ripped from me.

I gasped and shouted at the driver. Skip turned around and, in a flash, the motorbike disappeared from sight

Unfortunately, this is a pretty common occurrence in Phnom Penh. In a city rife with poverty, petty theft and bag snatching happens frequently. Fortunately, this is about as bad as it gets most of the time (unless you're inclined to party hard, toss back several cocktails and end up in a back alley at 3 am where anything could happen).

I have to say, though, I never felt unsafe at any time during our three years in Cambodia. Many a time, I walked home in the moonlight. I often meandered the dirt roads of small villages where nobody spoke a word of English. At no time did I feel threatened. After having my bag snatched, I took precautions and no longer carried a bag after dark (I used a fanny pack around my waist instead and didn't carry a lot of cash). I often took a tuk-tuk home instead of walking if it was late. But I never felt any of the concerns I sometimes experienced in big western cities that felt less safe and more threatening.

During our years living in Southeast Asia, we'd sometimes get comments from people back home. "Oh, you're so brave," a couple of them said. "I could never do what you do," said another." Don't you worry about your health?/the unstable political environment?/personal safety…?" But Skip and I both agreed there was nothing brave about living in Cambodia where we were surrounded by gentle, caring people who seemed more wired to laugh, give and share.

Road and train travel was a different story. Some of our greatest concerns were raised during long-distance trips (or even in crossing the road in Phnom Penh). Drivers in Southeast Asia aren't the most attentive or conscientious. They either drive at a snail's pace, holding up traffic while they turn a corner or park their minivans on a sidewalk, or they race along highways as if the devil was on their heels.

Our worst travel experience occurred during a trip to Vietnam where we took what we thought was the bus from Chau Doc to Canh Tho. It turned out to be one of many illicit bus companies that fool people into thinking they're the real thing. Skip and I piled on board the 12-seater with about 15 Vietnamese men, women and children. 15 minutes into the two-hour drive, we realized we'd made a big mistake. The young Vietnamese driver sped frantically along the highway, swerving around corners and yelling out of the window, causing all the passengers but us to throw up along the way. We held our breath, gripped our seats and eventually made it there safely—but we took the legit transportation on the way back (and learned to get better instructions for future travels).

Another time, we were on a bus returning to Phnom Penh from a long weekend in Ho Chi Minh City. We didn't realize it was the last day of a huge Cambodian holiday and that everyone would be on the road; traffic was horrendous. We got caught in a torrential rainstorm and the bus broke down at the ferry crossing, causing four skinny Cambodians to jump out of the bus and push it out of the mud. Fourteen hours later (it should have taken six) we arrived at our destination.

Another time, in a train station in India, waiting for an over-night train from Varanasi to Agra, I was heaving a heavy suitcase along the massively overcrowded station and across the railway bridge. A man approached and offered to carry my bag.

"I'm OK," I said, sweat running down my back and legs as I focused on the stairs ahead, gripping the handle of my case.

He persisted.

"No. I can manage." I snapped. I shoved through the crowds, up the stairs and left him in the dust.

"Pal, let her go," said Skip, laughing from a few paces behind. "It's going to end better for all of us if you just give up."

These experiences taught us: never expect things to go as planned, don't try to manage any situation, don't make plans that require tight scheduling and—as with everything having to do with travel in Asia—go with the flow. Above all, keep your sense of humor.

When it came to home security in Cambodia, we were warned about theft and break-ins, even in a second floor apartment. Robberies happened in some of the most creative ways. We heard stories of people coming home to find their wallets had been lifted through barred windows by thieves poking bamboo poles with sticky pads on the end to reach their targets.

The strangest robbery we experienced was when we awoke one morning to discover five bicycles missing from the front of our building. Since they had been behind a pair of eight-foot-high spiked and locked gates, someone had either scaled the gates or found a way to haul five bikes over them without disturbing anyone.

We never experienced anything worse than this but our friend, Matthew, had an expensive cell phone snatched from him while riding in a tuk-tuk, gave chase (not recommended when dealing with local robbers) and went to court to prosecute. One of our young Cambodian friends had a necklace ripped from her neck, also while in a tuk-tuk, and an American friend visiting from Thailand had her phone grabbed from her hand while walking in the street.

While there's a pretty high incidence of petty theft, being a victim is almost a rite of passage when you live in a city like Phnom Penh. Most of the expats shared horror stories and we learned from all of them.

It taught us to be aware, and not to carry much cash or flaunt jewelry or expensive cell phones, but it never made us concerned or afraid.

In some ways, it made us feel as though the onus was on us. Living in a country city where poverty is rife, there's sure to be petty crime, bag snatchings and theft, particularly around public holidays when extra money is needed by locals for travel to the provinces. We rarely heard of any violent crime against foreigners and didn't lose sleep worrying about anything more than an occasional mosquito buzzing around our heads. We also knew that, as westerners, we were often seen as walking ATMs and while we took precautions when we could, we felt that loss of "stuff" was not such a big deal as long as nobody was hurt.

11
A Shift in Thinking/Lessons Learned

*O*ur first Christmas in Cambodia was coming up. Local coffee
shops were decorated with shiny baubles and fake trees alongside traditional Buddhist shrines. Signs wishing "Happy Merry
Christmas" were hung outside shops and on the backs of tuk-tuks.
We'd been in Phnom Penh more than six months and didn't need—
or want—a thing. All our possessions fit into a couple of suitcases
and backpacks. We didn't want to weigh ourselves down or sink too
many roots that would be tough to pull up.

"What shall we buy ourselves for Christmas?" I asked Gabi
one morning.

Glancing at the back of my hand where the hair had been singed
off as I toasted slices of bread over an open flame on our stove every
morning, she replied, "How about we buy a toaster?"

Off we went to Orussey Market, a rabbit's warren of hot, crowded
aisles packed with tiny shop after boutique selling everything from

fish to clothing to bicycle parts to, well, toasters—a rare break from our "buy nothing" credo.

Toaster acquisitions aside, we've become non-consumers, instinctively rejecting impulses to buy where we once spent liberally. Our focus is on experiences, not things; enrichments, not riches.

"I didn't start living until I stopped consuming," fellow traveler and explorer John Bardos wrote to us. Like John, we have learned that less is indeed more. Possessing things vs. the potential of what might be is an attractive tradeoff.

Once I stopped thinking about financial security I was free to pursue an enriched life—a simple exercise for us once we got our brains around the idea of actually being homeless, migratory world residents. We are far from alone in this pursuit, having met countless others who have little by way of possessions but many lives' worth of enriching experiences.

It's been five years since we quit our jobs and embarked on a path toward something different. In the life ledger of gains and losses, the positives so outweigh the negatives that it's worth spending some time to enumerate and explain.

In that span of time we have learned a new culture, language and lifestyle as members of the Cambodian ex-pat community. We developed countless new, exciting friendships with fascinating people from all over the world with enormous commonality of thought and purpose, though from widely varying backgrounds. We've become completely at ease with being out of our element and in strange, sometimes mildly threatening situations. We now grow restless when we're in familiar environs for too long in the U.S. and England.

We traveled to roughshod places (rural Cambodia; flood-stricken Varanasi, India, and off the beaten path spots in Thailand, Vietnam and China) and in doing so opened up a world of travel opportunity.

Having been to these places and not just survived but flourished, we feel we can travel anywhere.

We have pushed our physical limits (me being chased by dogs while riding my bicycle in rural provinces and surviving two bouts of dengue fever and a double hit of malaria; Gabi, bumping along rut-strewn roads in Cambodia's outermost villages in cramped vans with no air conditioning, and finding peace with cheap, mosquito-infested guest houses on work-related trips). We found ways to create fulfilling, giving, meaningful and rewarding lives in a land more foreign than either of us could have imagined.

Some family and friends worried about our safety and health. Their concerns, although understandable and appreciated, were mostly unfounded. When confronted with difficulties and forced to adapt, we drew on nearby resources and people we knew and trusted, and leaned on each other to figure out our next steps. Not once did we consider packing up and heading back to the U.S.

We felt safer walking the streets of Phnom Penh, Hanoi, Bangkok and Saigon at all hours of the day and night than we often felt in Boston, New York, Los Angeles or Chicago. For the most part we went where and when we wished for our entire stint in Southeast Asia.

We often got lost, but some of our most amazing experiences came from taking a wrong turn or heading down unfamiliar roads that didn't exist on a map. I occasionally got sick, which complicated our lives and offered a different set of challenges, none more so than my bout of malaria in India.

Though pushing me to the edge of tolerance, this experience cemented our resolve; we could overcome just about any obstacles thrown our way. Living abroad gave us new capacity for resourcefulness and problem solving that we'd never thought possible.

A metamorphosis. Change.

Dramatic, and permanent.

Our values are different now. We appreciate the spirit of giving not as an act of "trickle down" financial matter, but as a visceral act of symbiotic humanity between one person and another.

We see the cost of living not as a price one pays to eat, rent or own, drive or use public transportation, bicycle or walk, but as the expense that goes with opening doors to opportunity and experience.

When we spend time in the west visiting family and friends, we are shocked by the speed, volume and cost of life back home. We are spoiled after living a life of reasonably priced places to live, access to delicious, clean and inexpensive food and low-cost travel while having all the comforts we would wish for within reach.

It's just the "things" that have gone from our lives. We consume less and acquire less.

But we have much, much more. Experiences, memories, knowledge, insight and a sense of being at ease in unfamiliar settings are powerful gifts in a quest for broader understanding. And at the risk of sounding like self-impressed travelers or narcissists, we feel we are better human beings for it.

The focus on "having," is replaced by the quest to "do." So, too, is the reactive competitive spirit in me that my hypnotherapist friend Mike once described as "an addiction to adrenaline."

Lower costs, combined with easy transfer of money from one country to another (mainly in the form of omnipresent ATMs on every street corner in every city in every country we have visited) make international personal finance a no-brainer.

Most important for us is how we feel about how we live, no matter where we are.

We are more comfortable in coffee shops in Hoi An where the chatter around us is in a language we don't understand than in a Starbucks on Boston's North Shore, surrounded by people with accents and language with which we are all too familiar.

I have become uncomfortable in my former home, a stranger in a familiar land.

We've been able to keep pace with global, national, regional and local events by setting up alerts on email and subscribing to news feeds that strike our fancy. We participate in elections by finding local organizations to help us cast ballots, and by creating connections with elections officials in the U.S. We continue to have a U.S. address—we use my sister's home—and file our taxes consistently on time, thanks to an accountant who knows us and works with us remotely.

I have developed a new appreciation for being a U.S. citizen. This odd sense of nationalist pride evolved as I met people of all walks of life from all over the world. We sometimes encountered people who were critical of U.S. policy and Americans' behavior and sometimes envious of the advantages that come with holding a U.S. passport and of the enormous range of personal choices that every U.S. citizen enjoys. Still, most of the people we encountered in the past five years expressed profound respect, gratitude and admiration for all the good things my country stands for.

Perhaps the most significant change we feel as a product of our journeys is our perception of and involvement in relationships: With other people. With other places. With money. The world is smaller, more accessible to us. We're accustomed to carrying five or six SIM cards for our phones, and several currencies at once. Language challenges are both a predictable obstacle to getting around and a convenient shield against exposure to the random chatter of strangers.

We've become more empathetic, smiling as a waiter delivers the wrong dish and laughing when a taxi driver conveniently drops us off in front of his cousin's shop. When things like that happen in our home countries, we find it irritating and difficult to tolerate.

We're still learning how to imbue this shift of thinking permanently into our lives. It's a matter of investing in self-compassion rather than self-esteem, as my friend Steve observed during one of our trips "back home." Stated otherwise, we've allowed ourselves to let go of what was. By doing so, we are both prepared to fully embrace the future.

I've let go of the trapeze, have completed the transition, and with my wonderful partner's hand in mine, eagerly look forward to what might be next.

Once complicated and woven into complex patterns, our lives are now centered around experiences, people and new connections. Having let go of many material goods and having found ways to maintain personal relationships back home, we're free to look forward and outward. Every day.

12
What Now?

O*h, 'Team Yetter is hard at work," said my friend Steve, descending in the morning to the first floor of his home and seeing Gabi and me at his dining room table, banging away at our laptops. "You guys are like travel machines."*

Although predisposed to living with no formal arrangements and no rules, walls or borders, Gabi and I have essentially created a two-shareholder Limited Liability Corporation that is owned, operated and staffed by Team Yetter. It's an alliance of shared goals, responsibilities and values with no org chart and no reporting structures. Oh, and no compensation, other than the richness of what we do, see and experience.

My ideal job, really.

We're co-CEOs, each assuming the role of boss at any moment. We take turns in these roles, each stepping up when the other has a down moment or seems in need of a bit of coddling.

While traveling in Peru in late 2014, after the second straight night of sleepless discomfort on the shores of Lake Titicaca, Gabi was uncharacteristically but understandably crabby. We were both struggling with the effects of altitude sickness, suffering from mild apnea (sudden cessation of breathing during sleep), slight headaches and chronic shortness of breath.

Besides the discomfort of being unable to easily walk distances or hustle up a flight of stairs, we were both deeply disappointed with Lake Titicaca, particularly with its lakeside hometown of Puno. (A rat hole of nondescript profile and history and one of the more inhospitable and boring places we've visited).

I was up and out the door of our hotel room just after sunrise, and after four cups of coffee and an hour and a half of research, I found the antidote for our ailments.

"Hey, I figured out our next move," I told Gabi, returning to our room and sitting on the side of the bed to welcome her to the morning. "It's a cool city a few hours away called Arequipa. I've read rave reviews about the city's history, architecture, restaurants and vibe—all good. Three volcanoes ring the city. And it's 1,000 meters lower than Puno."

"Sold," she said. Within an hour we were off to buy bus tickets.

🏃

"So, what's next?"

This is the number two question we are asked as we travel and meet people around the world and explain our choice of lifestyle. (The first being, "You're traveling now, but where is your home?")

The nice thing about being off the traditional treadmill is that once you're on your own path there's a lot of open space to trek.

Our nomadic lifestyle suits us, though we've had to learn tricks to adapt to climate fluctuations while traveling light. We now leave a cache of various clothes in the U.K. and U.S., supplementing with local purchase when necessary to avoid constant sweating or freezing to death. It's a tricky challenge, but we're getting the hang of it.

Despite my pride in simplifying, I now own three fleece jackets: One I absconded with from my Business Wire Days, a great vest that serves double duty while I am mountain biking on a chilly day in France; a mammoth pullover I got when I joined a health club in Massachusetts (which awaits return to our storage unit), and a lightweight North Face Chinese knockoff I bought while freezing my keister off in Dali, China. (Some duplicates make sense as long as you don't let it get out of hand.)

Take underwear, for example: I'm a lousy packer, often panicking before a trip and frantically cramming half of my possessions into a suitcase, only to realize I've left out the stack of essentials I carefully set aside in preparation for the trip. I'm prone to thoughtlessly adding stuff I won't need (think Steve Martin in The Jerk: "I need this … and I need this … and this….")

I temporarily lost my mind when we left for Cambodia, over-reacting to information I'd read about men who were unable to find clothing big enough for western bodies in Asia. I'm stuck with wide shoulders on a big frame, and having seen the tiny torsos on Thai men I figured I'd be having all my clothes custom made if I didn't go prepared. I packed six shirts, six pairs of pants and at least 30 pairs of underwear. Don't ask me why, and also don't ask me why I continue to ship the majority of my skivvies from country to country while carrying 6–8 pairs with me.

Like my revelation about dismounting from a life of work, it took modest behavioral change to get over my obsession with becoming "underwear challenged." Once I realized how easy it was to wash drawers in a hotel sink, the underwear conundrum became clear and very simple for me. (Though I'll admit a moment of doubt when, in Kunming, China, it was so cold and damp in our hotel room that nothing dried over the span of two days. I wound up standing in the corridor drying my underwear with the communal hair dryer that was bolted to the wall.)

We have since learned that the rest of the world has caught up to western sartorial demands. We can buy everything we want on the road—even underwear!

In nearly a year of constant travel in India, China, Thailand, Vietnam, England, France, the Netherlands, Belgium, Italy, Turkey, Cyprus and Greece, I've traveled with one medium suitcase and a backpack for my laptop, smart phone and current reading materials. Usually, I never get below the top layer of clothes in my suitcase, which would suggest that I am (a) manic and (b) a habitual over-packer. Both are probably fair assessments.

The important stuff of life is not in your suitcase or resting where you live, but what you do, see and create along the way. A suit in tow (you couldn't get me into one under any circumstances now, anyway) would be excess baggage for us to schlep around. So I don't. The only one I own remains hopelessly buried in the back of our storage cubicle. The only reason I hang on to it is that it's the suit I wore to our wedding. Call me a romantic sap; guilty as charged.

Traveling light makes it easy for us to be flexible—even irresponsible—in where we go and when. We filled three weeks of open space between house sits in France and Italy by taking a train from Marseille to Brussels, then drove to Bruges and up into The Netherlands for a peek at Utrecht, The Hague and Amsterdam before continuing along to Zwolle to meet up with a friend. Then we were off to wind our way to Switzerland to visit my niece and her family before continuing along to Italy for a house sit assignment two weeks later.

Short-term planning has become a ritual for us.

She: You know, we have no plans after (pick a month.)

Me: Hmmmm.

She: Any ideas?

Me: How about Spain … or Turkey … or Morocco? And off we go.

The roles are often reversed, but the process and outcome are largely unchanged. We count our blessings by being unencumbered by deadlines, expectations, plans or even considering the wishes of others. We've become adept at including family and friends in our travels, often meeting in cool places to hang for a few days (both my daughters and Gabi's nieces spent time with us during house sits in England and France, enjoying great personal time and a wonderful vacation in one shot.)

In 2013, we headed to South America, but since we only made it through Ecuador and Peru, we'll be back to see the rest. We're also casting an eye on Africa and other points on the world map where we've not touched down so far. For a year we meandered from house sit to house sit in England, France, Italy, Spain and Cyprus, learning about local cultures and assuming the lives of people who entrusted their homes and pets to us. I see our lives as a limitless photo album of boundless horizons, sunsets over oceans, mountains, valleys and vistas of all kinds. Our feet are up, revealing worn Tevas or sneakers. We are relaxed, taking in the wonder of it all, and considering the beauty of the world we embrace at every turn.

And we're smiling. Every day, nearly all the time. Many weeks, I'm not sure what day it is.

Best of all, Sundays are no longer loathsome beasts.

Section II
Stories from the
Other Side of Convention

13

W hen we left Massachusetts for Phnom Penh, we exchanged the familiar life for the unknown. Skip resigned from a good job. We sold our house and cars, opting for one-way airline tickets and a room in a cheap guesthouse. We said farewell to family and friends without any idea when we'd see them again. Some people were envious of the new life we were about to begin. Some challenged us and questioned our reasons for leaving. And some were concerned about our safety and wellbeing.

We had no idea what we were stepping into. And that had the biggest appeal of all.

Don't get me wrong. We weren't running from anything or unhappy with our lives in the U.S. Quite to the contrary; we lived in a beautiful area, had wonderful friends, travelled fairly frequently and had all the stuff that allegedly makes one happy. The funny thing is, in Cambodia we had all those same advantages—with the exception of the "stuff."

In Phnom Penh, we developed a special new network of friends, became involved with local communities, ate out, travelled often and felt every bit as safe (often more so) than we did back home.

The main difference: our lifestyle cost a fraction of what it did in the U.S.

We also learned we weren't alone in our untraditional lifestyle. We discovered boatloads of people just like us. We met them on our travels, bumped into them on buses and trains and found them on websites and Facebook groups dedicated to nomads, explorers and adventurers who'd said *adiós* or *sayonara* to their jobs, families and friends, and bought airline tickets or train passes to other parts of the world.

There were people in their 20s and their 50s. Some travelled solo; some travelled with a pack of kids in tow. Several had money in the bank; others had next to nothing. Some had portable businesses, some taught English, some had "location-independent careers" or did volunteer work and some started blogs or got by on freelance writing assignments. A number of them went for one year while others stayed for many. Some decided they didn't want to go home again. Some had a plan while others figured it out as they went. They were as varied as you'd imagine, and so were their stories.

40-something Barbara Adam describes herself as a "double dropout" while Adam Pervez (the "Happy Nomad") says he's been "happy and homeless for 918 days" (at the time of writing). The Miller family lost all their money in the stock market crash while they were in Italy. Talon Windwalker left home in 2011 with $900 in the bank and a nine-year old adopted son. Susan Spencer was unfulfilled in her high-powered job in San Francisco and made a life change that took her across the world. All had one thing in common: A desire to break away from what's considered a "normal lifestyle" and a yearning to plunge into something new, even if the idea may initially have been intimidating or daunting.

The following pages tell the stories of some of these intrepid souls and the lessons they've learned along the way. There are 20-somethings who discovered new perspectives on the world that we (in our 50s) were able to learn from, and mid-career professionals who traded monthly salary checks for an opportunity to volunteer their services in third-world countries. One woman in her 50s decided to join the U.S. Foreign Service. Some people who felt they didn't fit in created lives for themselves (and often for their kids as well) in gentler, more economically friendly parts of the world.

We've organized these anecdotes into categories to reflect the subjects' ages and stages of life.

While their ages vary and most come from different economic backgrounds, their stories contain powerful messages. We encourage you to read them all. It's possible that you—like us—may learn something from someone 20 years your junior or senior. A few have personal blogs and websites you can read for more information on how they did it and how you, too, can make changes in your life (listed at the end of this section).

.

14
I'm Young and Fancy Free

*A*dam Pervez first hit the road when he was 22. Ten years later, he describes himself as being "happy and homeless for 918 days." The spark was ignited when he took a 10-day study abroad trip to Egypt during college, where he was studying electrical and computer engineering, and realized for the first time that "all it takes to see the amazing wonders in this world is a little bit of money, a plane ticket and an open mind."

Returning to his final term at college after the Egypt trip, Adam looked for work that would provide international exposure. He took a job as a field engineer for an oil services company that took him to Abu Dhabi, Scotland and Qatar. He earned excellent money and travelled quite a bit but soon discovered "money wasn't everything and the lifestyle of a field engineer in the oil industry wasn't for me.

He signed up for business school in Madrid, completed an MBA and started working as a business development specialist with Siemens Wind Power in Denmark, which he felt would "help me atone for the environmental sins committed in the oil industry."

However, the high-powered job and big salary didn't do it for him. "I realized that I would never be happy with what everyone else considers a normal life," he said. "I needed to live a life based on my passions, not one based on maximizing income.

"I had achieved exactly what I'd set out to do, but realized it wasn't what I wanted. I was following a script for success written by someone else, or by society. And the corporate world just wasn't for me. It's too stressful, political and unfulfilling. I felt I could never make much of an impact on the world from behind my desk in comfortable Denmark, so I looked within, found what my true calling was and "took the plunge."

In 2011 he quit his job and made the decision to explore the world. He launched a website named The Happiness Plunge and embarked on the *Happy Nomad Tour,* starting in Mexico while focusing on volunteering, writing, teaching, telling stories and learning about other cultures and what makes them happy. "'The Happy Nomad' is what I came up with after identifying my passions of traveling, writing and helping others through teaching, learning and telling stories," he said. "I'm truly happy and I'm truly a nomad."

Adam began his trip in Mexico then took buses through Central and South America. He then moved to Southeast Asia, followed by Nepal and India, Eastern Europe, the Middle East and Africa. He volunteers his services everywhere he goes with the goal of leaving each place better than it was when he found it. "Taking the plunge was a shortcut to get me on the fast track to giving myself a fighting chance at reaching my full potential in life," he said. "I knew as a 28-year-old single guy, it was now or never. Life often gets more complicated as you get older, so I thought it would be best to take the shortcut then when I was healthy and had no baggage.

"I also realized, after lots of internal deliberation trying to figure out what was wrong with me, that nothing was wrong with me. **I just wanted something different out of life and if I didn't go after it now, I might never get the chance. For me, happiness is being in love with life.**"

His family was "supportive, but not thrilled" as they were concerned for his safety. Friends were encouraging as most figured it was going to be "a year of vacation or something, not a change in lifestyle."

"For many of them there was no gray area between backpacker bum and corporate tool/slave," he said. "But I am debt-free and living off the money I earned in Denmark. I wrote a monthly article for the *Singapore Business Times,* which brought in some income and am now in the process of starting a consultancy in the U.S. to help companies measure their happiness and train them in how to provide happier workplaces."

As Adam planned his next move, a friend recommended *The Art of Non-Conformity* by Chris Guillebeau, which became "the chicken soup for my soul."

"As I read, it felt as though flowers that had been inside me since birth finally received some sunlight and water and sprang to life. I felt more and more energetic and motivated. It got things moving in a positive direction; I knew an unconventional life was right for me. Much of the stress and dismay in my life was due to the fact that I am not cut out for a conventional life. And knowing this, knowing that I'm just different, totally changed my perspective. It was empowering.

"After a lot of thought and contemplation, I realized my passions included learning/teaching, helping others and telling stories so I planned my journey around these passions. For the first time in a long time I felt alive. I felt excited and enthusiastic. I had a purpose, goals and a new adventure.

"There is no perfect time to take the plunge. The stars will never align perfectly. You have to go out and do the work and make it happen. I had to figure out what I am passionate about and the rest was easy."

So what was Adam's long-term vision and personal narrative? "My vision includes living a simple life full of non-conformity, doing the things I love most and never failing to be curious about everything around me."

"Don't expect it to be easy. Everyone has their stuff to get over and conquer, so don't compare yourself or your trip to others. Just go at your pace, enjoy every moment and take nothing for granted. I've never been happier. I've become much more spiritual, more confident, independent, resilient and extroverted. It's been quite a journey!"

Over the past couple of years, Adam has been offering career and life coaching as well as speaking at universities with a focus on "inspiring students to think outside the box and pursue careers aligned with their personal goals and ambitions." His long-term goal is to complete a Ph.D. program in positive psychology and teach positive leadership.

Meghan Coleman and Eliza Chute had never met one another until they arrived in Cambodia. Along with us, they'd both signed up for VIA (Volunteers In Asia), an American organization which places volunteers throughout Southeast Asia, and found themselves working for the same NGO in Phnom Penh, both learning Khmer and figuring out how to get used to squat toilets and potholed roads. After two years, Eliza moved to

Thailand to work for a human rights organization. Her plan is to pursue a JD/MBA so she can study and work in the field of international corporate social responsibility. Meghan returned to the U.S. to complete an MBA in social entrepreneurship and worked with an impact investment firm in Colorado before taking off on a six-month sojourn to South America and Asia.

"I always knew I wanted to spend a year abroad after college," said Eliza. "In the beginning I found life in Cambodia to be quite challenging. I oscillated between being sad and homesick and ecstatic. It was an emotional rollercoaster at first, but after a while I found my feelings evened out. As time went on I came to love living in another country. My one year turned into two then three and now I'm not sure when I'll live in the U.S. again."

Eliza went to Cambodia at the age of 22 and spent a year living in rural areas working for an agricultural NGO. After her job ended, she moved to Thailand for two years, then traveled to Australia, Indonesia, Singapore, Thailand, the U.S., Western Europe, Taiwan and Vietnam.

"A lot of people told me I was really brave to move abroad but that always perplexed me, as it wasn't a scary thing to me at all. I wanted go overseas and I was excited to be there, so I don't feel I deserved to be called brave.

"I think it's good to get a different perspective on the world and see how other people live when you're in your 20s. There are so many more meaningful things that people value abroad that are overlooked when you're caught up in the rat race in the U.S. "I found that, for a lot of people, the idea of leaving home and going to live somewhere completely different was very exciting, but they were stuck in their current lives and didn't know how to make such a dramatic change. I have friends who are always saying they want to travel and live abroad, but they never actually do it. My best advice would be **JUST DO IT.** The world isn't really all that scary once you get out there. And in some ways, it's much easier than living in the States."

For Meghan, her trip to Cambodia at the age of 26 wasn't designed to change her life, but to add something new and expand her horizons.

"Living abroad and working in international development were two things I had aspired to since I transitioned to the nonprofit world and decided to dedicate my career to social justice and change," she said. "My perception (whether right or wrong) was that the need of underserved communities was greater in countries like Cambodia where poverty levels were extreme and social/institutional support systems were not in place to provide aid.

"After a nasty relationship breakup in which I abandoned all personal aspirations and goals, I was ready to make a dramatic life change. I was ready to challenge myself and have an adventure."

Books such as *The Art of Happiness* by the Dalai Lama and *The Soul of Money* by Lynne Twist were influential in her life, as were classes on Southeast Asian studies and global social and sustainable enterprise.

"Reactions from my friends and family about moving abroad were mixed. Some people were excited, but mostly people were fearful of what they didn't know about this new exotic place I would come to call a second home. This was never more evident than when my company threw a going away party for me and showered me with gifts of mosquito nets, rape whistles, emergency radios and water filters."

Her year spent in Cambodia, working in communications and fundraising, made her feel "alive for one of the first times in my life."

"It was refreshing to live in a place where people weren't defined or made happy by what they owned, but by who they loved, how they supported one another and how hard they worked. Life was a constant adventure. Whether I was navigating the local bus system to visit a rural province for the weekend or simply taking a bike ride down the street to pick up fruit from the market, I was challenged and engaged."

After Cambodia, Meghan returned to the U.S. to complete an MBA program in global social and sustainable enterprise. During that time, she spent three months in Nairobi exploring the development of a fortified porridge for malnourished children in urban slums in East Africa. This experience subsequently led her to co-found MamaCarts, a food cart micro-franchise in West Africa . After returning once again to the U.S., she got a job working at an impact investment company in Denver targeting innovative business creation and market-rate investments that increase the health, education and wellbeing of low-income children in Colorado. It took a while for her to settle back into U.S. life, however as she encountered a number of challenges after living and working in Southeast Asia.

"The biggest difficulty I faced was in interacting with friends and family," she said. "It was difficult to share my experiences in a way people could relate to. I eventually stopped telling my 'this one time in Cambodia' stories except to others who had lived abroad. American friends had no context for making those stories relevant.

"While abroad I also developed contempt for the hyper-consumerism and materialism of Western culture; so much so that it was difficult not to be judgmental when I came back. It has taken a few years to strike a good personal balance. I am happy now knowing that I can live with much less and be content.

"Most importantly, this experience widened my world view and helped me put what is important in life into perspective (not that I don't still get caught up in trivial things). I carry that with me every day, and I'm excited for the day when I decide pull the trigger and make the move again." (At the time of this writing, Meghan is traveling in South America and Asia).

John Bardos was 27 when he first left his home in Canada in 1997 to move to Japan with no job and no work visa on a week's notice.

"When I first left Canada, it was mainly because I needed a major life change. After university, I had very little interest in working at a low level position in a large corporation. My attempts at running my own business had failed, and I needed to reset my life. Moving abroad was the best way to accomplish that, so I bought a ticket to Japan with nothing planned and about $1,000 to my name.

"I expected to be there for only six months but, within two years of teaching English and no plans to leave, I married a wonderful Japanese woman and we decided to start our own school. We invested everything we owned and it started working out really quickly. Life was good for the first four or five years. However, while our business was successful and we had the money to buy the things we wanted, we didn't feel challenged or fulfilled. Growing the business stopped being enjoyable. New staff and growth brought administrative headaches. We thought new possessions would make us happy but our lives were stagnating and our dreams were disappearing.

"To fill that void, we did what everyone does—we went shopping. We bought the house we wanted, upgraded our car, bought the espresso machine, built the sound room with Italian reclining chairs, drank the expensive alcohol, went out for dinner every day and travelled a lot.

"Every new purchase and experience brought some fleeting excitement, but it never lasted. We always needed something a little more or a little better to be fulfilled.

"All the conveniences and luxuries I thought I needed to make me successful were actually making me fat, lazy and stupid. I drank too much, ate too much, watched too much TV, didn't exercise enough, didn't read as much as I liked and didn't spend my time doing what I most wanted to do.

"My body and mind were gradually deteriorating through misuse, yet I didn't think anything of it. I felt like I was successful despite my unhappiness and general lethargy. It took me a long time to realize that my ingrained definition of success was the problem."

In 2009, they made a one-year plan to sell their business, car, house and possessions and live a nomadic life of travel. On his blog, Jetsetcitizen, he wrote: "My wife and I really want to experience other cultures and challenge ourselves professionally. To that end, we have decided to leave our secure business and lifestyle and try something different in a new country. We are both about 40 years old so this may be our last chance to really start over. We have enough savings to survive for a few years, but we are not rich by any stretch of the imagination. We feel we are very close to the age limit of being able to lose everything and still have a chance at a secure old age."

Since letting go of his work and possessions, John and his wife have spent time in Turkey, Thailand, Hungary, Singapore, Malaysia, the UK, Germany, Austria, Italy, Switzerland and Australia. He's done numerous volunteer projects and freelance marketing consulting as well as built various websites. While at times he likes the idea of having a home base, the nomadic life-style makes him happy. He describes himself as being "location independent" since 2010.

"Leaving Japan was very different from leaving Canada. I was married, had a good business, a house, a car and all the posses-sions I wanted. My wife and I were making a good income, had lots of time and freedom to travel, and had achieved a good life. It would have been very easy to continue on that path for the next 10 or 20 or 30 years until retirement.

"We didn't want that to be the end of our story, but we were afraid to change. We worried about our financial security. We were concerned about the quality of our retirement. All those fears kept us paralyzed for years. Our life was good, but we felt there was more out there to do and explore. So many people are afraid to commit to anything just because they imagine some better opportunity will be coming soon. I believe we make our own opportunities and more often than not, they come from focusing our energies on one single job or business."

After changing his life a second time, John and his wife say they are happier than ever in living an inexpensive lifestyle of fewer possessions.

"We have more time to exercise, eat healthy home-cooked meals, spend time with friends and family, volunteer and work on projects of our own choosing. We will continue this as long as we can, while living in different parts of the world.

"We live in a time of great affluence and opportunity. It is easy and cheap to travel around the world, start new businesses and even become famous if we are willing to put in the work and are able to commit our energies to a single focus. **The greatest times in my life have been when I didn't have much money, didn't have many possessions and was working insane hours to accomplish something.** The "good life" is not necessarily an easy life. 'Easy' makes us fat and lazy. Even if you completely fail, there are unlimited opportunities to start again. Our parents never had these opportunities. Our grandparents couldn't have imagined this level of wealth and choice. There is no excuse for not attempting great things in life. The only barrier is our own fear, which is generally unfounded, and our unwillingness to do the work required.

"For many years of my life, I felt that success came through economic wealth and conspicuous consumption. It took me a long time to realize those things are not important. Without good health and rich personal relationships, life isn't worth much, yet so many of us have so much debt and financial obligations that we don't have time for what is most important. **I didn't start living until I stopped consuming.**

"Life is short. If you are not doing what you want now, then when? Doubling the size of your house is not going to make you twice as happy. In fact, it will add stress because you'll work more to pay for it, shop more for furniture, tools and accessories and spend more time on maintenance, cleaning and other chores. It is impossible to buy your way to a satisfying life."

15
Hitting 30 and Open To Change

When **Barbara Adam** *(The Dropout Diaries)* went on a cycling holiday through Vietnam and Cambodia at the age of 36, she never imagined it would change her life. Working as a political journalist in Australia, she wasn't unhappy with her job; she was just unhappy with the "all consuming nature of it." Today, she lives in Ho Chi Minh City, is married to a Vietnamese man, has two children and owns a company with him.

"In 2006, I decided to take a 'holiday of a lifetime trip' and booked a cycling holiday through Vietnam and Cambodia. My dad joined me for the first part and, when I got back to Australia, he was on a huge high from having had such a wonderful holiday. I, on the other hand, had a very bad case of post-holiday blues. My real life didn't seem worthwhile anymore.

"I had an epiphany at a party in Canberra shortly afterward. I was full of excitement about what I'd seen and done but everyone

at the party was focused on their jobs. They were mostly journalists and sometime after midnight I realized that the same
work-related conversation was still going on—after six hours!
This was my future if I continued to climb the ladder in the
Australian media. I started looking for a way out the next day."

The next step for Barbara was to quit her job, buy an airline
ticket back to Asia and take an ESL (English as a Second
Language) teaching course in Ho Chi Minh City. After completing the course, she taught for a while but didn't enjoy it, so she
travelled around northern Vietnam and Laos before taking a
job with an English language newspaper in Ho Chi Minh City.

A few months later, she met and fell in love with a Vietnamese
man. They got married and decided to start a family. She lost
her job shortly after her daughter was born and decided to
take a post in Singapore in order to be a "responsible parent."
Singapore didn't work out so Barbara decided to drop out once
again. She moved to Chiang Mai, Thailand, for seven months
then returned to Vietnam where she and her husband started a
business offering street food tours. In January, 2014, she gave
birth to her second child.

"In Australia, I'd been earning a good living and worked in
a job that gave me a corporate credit card. It was interesting
seeing the high life but I didn't feel it made up for the soul-de-
stroying nature of the job.

"I earn far less at the moment and I have virtually no 'stuff' but I am much happier. I have fallen out of the cycle of consumerism, and I think that is one of the biggest benefits of my dropouts. At the moment I am working part time and making enough to support my family and I'm setting up the business to run as a part-time concern so we can enjoy our little ones while they are little."

Luckily for Barbara, her friends and family were supportive of her move ("even the people who thought I was throwing my life and career away"). Any obstacles she encountered were internal. "My biggest obstacle was fear—fear of the consequences and a deep anxiety that I would run out of money and end up dressed in rags, crouching in a gutter with suppurating sores, begging passers-by for scraps of bread.

"Between making the decision to quit my job and leaving Australia, I spent many sleepless nights worrying about the most outlandish what-if situations. In hindsight it was a complete waste of energy. None of the things I was worried about eventuated and the less-than-positive experiences I've had I dealt with with hardly any fuss. Like many people, I am often my own worst enemy.

"The first time I dropped out of the rat race I only had to worry about myself and ensure I had enough of a cushion to buy a flight back to Australia. The second time I dropped out, I had a family to support. Now I need enough of a cushion to pay a few months rent and buy tickets for all of us back to Australia. "But my experience shows that it is possible to have a fulfilling life that's not the life society expects of you. I met society's school-university-work-hard-and-climb-the-ladder expectation and never felt fulfilled. Life is not perfect now; I have my share of down days, anxiety and worry about the future. But I am far happier now, working part time, owning very little stuff, experiencing a foreign culture and focusing on my family—a family I never expected to have and probably wouldn't have had if I hadn't dropped out.

"I had a mini-epiphany once at a funeral when I listened to people describing the deceased's life and wondered 'How do I want to be remembered?' If I dropped dead right then, the following week my friends and family would gather and talk about how I worked very hard and loved my dog like a child.

"Fast forward a few years and my beloved dog is gone; I have two children. I've traveled, worked in four countries, written a book, started a business and done all kinds of other exciting things. My life is much more fulfilling than when I was dedicated to my career."

Diana Edelman rrealized at age 30 there was nothing to tie her down. She was bored with her job as Director of Communications for a restaurant group and describes her state of mind as being in a "30 Life Crisis."

Her desire for discovery started in 2010 when she quit her job in Atlanta and went on a solo seven-month backpacking adventure through Europe and Africa—the longest period she'd ever been out of the U.S. On her blog (DTravelsRound), she wrote "The past six months I have breathed with more passion, more life, more love than I have ever done before. I have learned more about me, learned to like me more—more than I ever have before."

She returned home a changed person. She wrote of the day she returned: "I closed my eyes, letting the memories from my time abroad rush over me one last time. Then I grabbed my bag and exited the plane. I followed the throngs of people to the mobile lounge that takes passengers from the international gates to customs. I was deafened by the sounds around me: phones ringing, people talking into handsets, Blackberrys and iPhones. "I thought, Oh. My God. What are these people doing? Had I been one of those people before my trip?

"I sat and stared, thinking there was no way in the world after leaving Europe I would want to tarnish the memories by picking up a phone. The last thing I wanted to do was look at e-mails or talk shop. I wanted to savor every minute detail of my time there: the places, the beauty, the people. A life that pulses with electricity, passion and love makes nearly every other experience dull by comparison."

After a few months, she relocated to Las Vegas but wanderlust was still tearing a hole in her soul and demanding attention. So, in September, 2011, she booked a two week trip to Thailand to visit the Elephant Nature Park in Chiang Mai, quit her job five months later to become a freelance travel writer and was offered a position the following month handling writing and PR for the elephant park. She moved to Thailand in July 2012. "I decided to make my big change because Las Vegas wasn't doing it for me anymore. I am fortunate enough to be able to write anywhere in the world, and even more fortunate to have the opportunity to help Save The Elephant Foundation in Thailand. I was not happy with the life I was living in the U.S. I wanted to get back in touch with myself and be able to live for me, my dreams, my passions. I am able to do that in Thailand without worrying about paying the bills, driving a car, commuting to work … it is a far more laid-back life. For nearly a year before moving to Thailand, I was severely depressed. I was working through it and, when I finally came to love myself, I realized I owed myself a chance to live my life the way I chose. My parents were extremely supportive of my move. They encouraged me every step of the way, even though it meant having me halfway around the world. Some of my friends were supportive but others asked me what I was thinking and told me I was nuts."

Through her work writing freelance articles and from a small blogging income, Diana made more than enough to live in Thailand where the cost of living is low. While she knows this move took her in the direction of her heart, it wasn't without challenges along the way.

"The biggest challenge was being lonely. As far as meeting other native English speakers goes, most of them in this town are fairly transient. And because I volunteer and do freelance work, it is hard to go out and meet people. It is even more complicated because I walk or bus it everywhere so I can't always get to places outside the neighborhood. But my greatest delight is walking up and back to work every day and seeing everything around me—and spending time with the elephants at Elephant Nature Park.

"It's difficult to meet men in this town as they are more interested in dating Asian women. This is probably the most difficult thing about living in Thailand. It isn't a disappointment, just one of those things which allow me to take more time for me and to focus on my health and wellness.

"I can't envision ever living in America long-term again. I love my country, but don't love living there. It isn't for me anymore. After being in Southeast Asia for so long, and living far more basically, my norms and desires have changed. I have grown far more accustomed to the gritty than the polished. **I prefer to explore the world and take up residence in a place where the routine is no routine.**

"I wake up every day feeling ridiculously blessed. Being in Thailand has allowed me to look at things differently. Things I would never do in America, things I would not accept as a way of living in America, I accept here. If I want to walk down the street barefoot, I do. If I get a dirty plate, I wipe it off instead of sending it back. I'm working on adopting the Thai attitude of 'no worries.' Since I have been here, my mind has opened so much. The culture here is very different than that of the western world, and while I don't always agree with everything, it has been eye opening to learn about it and accept it. I have become a more conscious person in terms of the decisions I make and how they impact other living beings.

"My message to other people who think about making a change in their lives would be: Take the risk. Live your life as you see fit, not how others expect you to live. Follow your heart. Follow your dreams. It works out. **Life's not about living happily ever after … it's about living.**"

Ate Hoekstra was 31 when he left his hometown of Leeuwarden in The Netherlands to pursue a dream of working as a freelance journalist in Asia. He'd been working two jobs—one as a communications specialist at a government agency and the other as a freelance journalist—when a three-month work stint as a volunteer editor in China in 2009 gave him a taste for travel. In June 2012, he booked a flight to Phnom Penh, Cambodia. He has been finding freelance work and travelling around Southeast Asia ever since.

"Back then I had a job as a clerk in an office, but decided to go back to college to study journalism. Three years later in 2009 I graduated and left home for the first time. I went to Shanghai to do an internship with the magazine That's Shanghai and came back home three months later. In The Netherlands it was easy to find a good job, but it didn't feel right to sit in an office all day and watch the world go by. I wanted to be part of it. I wanted to explore the world. I knew there was more to life.

"Meanwhile things were not going well with journalism. Many editors and journalists were getting fired and it seemed as though everybody was working as a freelancer which meant there was much more competition unless you were specialized in something. When I came back from a backpacking trip throughout Singapore and Malaysia, I knew what to do: Leave home, move to Southeast Asia, work hard and make the best of it. About eight months later that's exactly what I did.

"Most of my family and friends supported me, but some didn't understand. Why was I leaving? I had a good job, a nice house, enough money to go on a holiday twice a year. And I wanted to give all that up for some uncertain future in the undeveloped world? Someone told me I could easily find a job as a reporter for the local newspaper. It was impossible to make him understand that wasn't an option at all.

"Some people criticized the idea because they thought it would be impossible to make a living working as a freelancer in Southeast Asia. They were wrong. I'm happy I didn't let their opinion change my plans.

"Going abroad is one of the best things I've done. It changed my mind, my way of thinking, my view on the world. It's easy to have an opinion based on what you see on the TV back home, but it's so much more interesting to turn off the TV and explore the world yourself. We humans are made to travel and explore new horizons. It opens your mind—and the more open your mind is, the more you start to appreciate life. Back home many people say they want to travel the world or live abroad for some time. But they believe it's not possible because of a job, a house, a marriage or a few kids. I think anything is possible. **You just have to do it.**"

Nora Dunn, aka **The Professional Hobo,** sold her successful financial business in Toronto and hit the road in 2007 at the age of 30 to travel the world.

"I was what you could call a 'medium-sized fish in a big pond,' having achieved a certain level of success and a reputation for helping people engineer their finances to enable their life's dreams. I regularly appeared on television, gave interviews in newspapers opposite financial "celebrities" and spoke in front of audiences as large as 3,000 people.

"But something wasn't right. A little voice inside me—a voice that has been a lifelong friend or pest, depending on how you look at it—said *"Nora ... you're not doing what you're supposed to be doing. There's something else out there for you."* I realized that in helping my clients achieve their dreams and goals, I'd forgotten my own dream of long-term immersive travel."

In January of 2006, Nora was in two car accidents in one week. Several months later, she suffered two bouts of bronchitis that developed into walking pneumonia.

"People said 'the Universe is trying to tell you something,' but I was annoyed at this diagnosis. *'What is the Universe trying to tell me, for goodness sake? That I shouldn't drive in the snow Get outta my way; I've got work to do.'"*

"It wasn't until I developed pneumonia that I was forced to stop everything for a spell. Shortly thereafter, the ball dropped. There were so many things I wanted to do; I knew I couldn't achieve these goals in the way I truly wanted with week-long—or even month-long—vacations. I had to go deeper than that. It had to be a lifestyle."

A savings account and the sale of her business provided Nora with a small income for the following 2 ½ years. Her intention was to travel during that time, then return to the working world "re-energized and enthused."

"I'll never forget the day I walked into the office to meet with my divisional and regional directors. I had garnered some attention in the financial planning industry, and specifically within the company I worked for, so I wasn't particularly surprised when my announcement of plans to sell my practice and go off to "play" in Costa Rica (an arbitrarily-chosen first destination) was met with open mouths and wide eyes.

"'See, I told you' ', said Bill the regional director, to my division director when he recovered from the initial shock. "I knew something was up.

"'Tell you what we're going to do," he said. "We're going to manage your business for you. Go do what you need to do, for six months, a year, whatever. When you get it out of your system, you can come back and step right back into your life here.'

"It was a tempting offer. After six long hard years of work, I was earning six figures, and had reached the point in my business where I could follow a trend of working less and earning more. In many ways I had done all the hard work of building up a business without fully reaping the rewards. If all I had to do was "get something out of my system", then this arrangement would have been ideal. Traveling with the security of knowing there is something to come home to can be a wonderful safety net, especially if you're not sure what you're looking for or what you'll find.

"However, instead of seeing this offer as a 'safety net,' I saw it as a limiter. How could I embrace whatever was on the road for me to discover if I knew I had to come back to a life so stressful for me that I burnt out mentally and physically from it? And how did I know that when I came back, I'd even want to live in the same city?

"I was looking for a fresh start. Having anything tying me to 'home' was difficult to comprehend; everything had to go: the business, the car, the motorcycle, the skydiving gear, the chic urban loft on the beach and all the 'stuff' that was inside it. In so doing, I was letting go of the traditional definition of 'home' in its entirety, knowing that letting go would reveal a new definition of 'home' and a new way of life."

Since leaving Canada, Nora has visited more than 40 countries, written a book—*How to Get Free Accommodation Around the World*— done volunteer work and written freelance articles for a variety of publications.

In 2010, she kept a detailed log of her expenses travelling in Australia, New Zealand, Spain, England, Ireland, Germany, France and Nepal. Her expenses included accommodation, travel, medical costs, an iTouch purchase, professional work on her website, food, hiking gear, car rental, entertainment, flights and health insurance.

At times, her expenses were low (such as in New Zealand) where she was provided with free accommodation in exchange for volunteering). While some of her costs were lower when she shared them with a partner, her average daily expenses were as follows: Australia: $53, New Zealand: $25; Spain: $32; Germany: $62; France: $39; UK: $61; Ireland: $69; France and Nepal: $11 (where she was filming a travel television show pilot and her expenses were covered). Her total expenditure for 2010 was $17,271. (see What Does It Cost?, Chapter 22)

"I was no scrooge on my travels. I spent money when I wanted to spend money, I bought new clothes, I ate dinners out and I enjoyed the company of friends in a number of scenarios—from drinking to hiking to sightseeing to attending festivals.

"But in keeping my overall costs low by staying with friends, volunteering, and employing some clever travel hacks such as using frequent flyer miles, getting free accommodation through volunteering or house-sitting, and knowing the right ways and places to search for flights and accommodation, my cost of full-time travel was considerably less than any full year I spent living a conventional life in Canada. And my location independent income as a writer more than covered my living expenses.

"When you employ creative slow-travel strategies, full-time travel just doesn't have to be that expensive. **I've consistently spent less money to travel full-time than I ever did living in one place.**"

Laurel Avery had been considering a move to Europe for years but the final push came for her when George Bush was elected President.

"The fact that the U.S. population was so apathetic that they either did not vote or didn't care to contest what was obviously a stolen election made me want to leave the rats to the sinking ship. The timing was right as I was not in a relationship, had no family obligations and was working for myself. I had built a house in Santa Fe that did not go well, my financial situation was deteriorating quickly and I felt it was time for a change."

Laurel (37 at the time) worked as a freelance graphic designer and editor for publishers in the U.S. She decided to spend a year in Paris working as an artist to see if it could develop into something more. She managed to sell enough of her artwork to keep going for a while, then decided to transition into a more practical field which included writing and editing.

"Most everyone was very supportive of my move. My family (basically my mother and grandmother) was already living far enough away that I only got to visit them once a year or so anyway, so it was not a big change for them. And my friends were happy for me, if a tad jealous. The most interesting remark I continually heard was 'I'd love to do something like that, but couldn't do it myself.' My opinion was 'of course you could!'

"We all make choices. My choice was to give up my (way too big) expensive house in exchange for a cheap flat in France, sell my car and leave my friends for a life I felt would be better. They chose to keep their high-paying 9 to 5 jobs, their fancy cars and expensive homes. There was nothing making them do that; it was just the choice they made.

"The funniest thing was talking to my best friend on Skype, who would ask me 'When are you coming home?' to which I always replied, 'I *am* home!'

When Laurel left the U.S., her house had been on the market for a year-and-a-half with no offers so she took out a home equity loan to cover the costs of the year she planned to spend abroad.

"Though I had visited France nearly every year for the previous 10 years on two-week vacations, I knew visiting a place and living in it could be two different things. I figured I would give it a year and see how I liked actually living there. If at the end of that time I decided it was not for me, I could always return to the U.S."

She didn't. After living in France for four years, Laurel moved to Spain for three years then to the Netherlands where she lives with her partner and their three-year-old daughter and has a family business that offers medical writing, editing and translating from Spanish to English.

"We had a difficult couple of years, but the past year-and-a-half has been much better. I have become well established and have a number of good-paying steady clients, which means I can work less and have more time to pursue my own creative projects. "The greatest challenges had to do with dealing with bureaucracy and the almost total lack of customer service here. Though I don't like the way many things are done in the U.S., at least it's easy to accomplish day-to-day things, such as changing an address, getting an appliance fixed, having a plumber come in, etc. Things are not done very efficiently in Europe, and though I have gotten pretty used to it by now, it still bothers me from time to time.

"And the fact that it is not easy to make friends here doesn't help. I have managed to find friends through the expat community, both in France and Spain, though I have been able to make almost no close friends anywhere who were not Anglophones. I speak French decently, but the French all seem to make their friends while growing up, and if you haven't made them by the time you're 20, that's it for you. I suppose no matter where I live here, I will always be a foreigner.

"Nevertheless, I love living here. I share more of the same values with Europeans than I ever shared with my fellow Americans. I like the slower pace of life, enjoying days off, not worrying about a lack of healthcare, bike-friendly roads, the way children are cared for, the lack of a juvenile viewpoint toward sex, and the excellent public transportation systems (except for the Netherlands).

"We have no fears of going bankrupt from medical bills or being unable to pay for our daughter's education in Europe. We pay a little over 100 Euros ($130) a month for medical care, which covers most things except elective surgeries and pharmaceuticals (which are usually very reasonably priced).

"Although there is no question that moving from one's home country is stressful, it was without a doubt the best thing I could have done for my personal growth and happiness. Life in Europe is more balanced, its citizens enjoy a (very good) basic level of care that ensures a good living standard and there is not the level of fear here that one sees in the U.S. If you turn on a TV here you are not bombarded with the latest 'homicide/killer bees/terrorists in the back garden' story that you are in America. And every other commercial is not for a pharmaceutical product.

"I don't envision ever returning to the U.S., but I wouldn't rule it out. When I was going to university in New York I always thought I might end up as an elderly woman there (or perhaps in the Berkshires), but I see that less and less. Seeing how my life has taken me so many different places, I can't even begin to imagine where I might end up.

"To anyone who has ever considered living abroad, I'd say go ahead and do it! The worst that can happen is you won't like it, and you go back to your home country. Whatever happens, it will enrich your life."

16
Experienced and Keen to Explore

With a doctorate in International and Multicultural Education from the University of San Francisco and more than 25 years of experience as a licensed mental health therapist and college instructor, **Dr. Ryan James** was unable to find a suitable position in any state in the U.S. he was willing to live. In 2001, at the age of 47, after sending out hundreds of CVs and receiving no positive responses, he decided to take off with his partner, now legal spouse, Ron Schmitz, to travel for a year. "We had redecorated the house about a year earlier, as an attempt to renew my feelings about staying where we were, but it did not work. We sold all our major things using a silent auction, but I kept 4,000 books and 95% of the things we had collected from past travels. We sold our cars, rented out the house, and, most painfully, adopted out our dog.

"When the decision was made to take off, I put an end to all shopping (which I loved to do). Between the two of us, we had about $11,000 in credit card debt so I put each of us on a strict budget, and planned a year ahead to get rid of the debt and have money in the bank. By the time we left, we had no credit card debt, the vehicles were sold and the house was rented. There was $10,000 in the bank. Ron took early retirement and, due to his years of working for the same agency, didn't lose anything in terms of benefits. He held off on Social Security and relied solely on his pension. Our plan was to teach English as needed to stretch the money."

Ryan and Ron travelled to Europe, exploring multiple countries before settling in Hungary after they made a stop there to hunker down for the winter. Ryan taught for 12 years at Eötvös Loránd University—the last six years as Coordinator of the Journalism/Writing Program—as well as working as a freelance writer for travel publications and operating a mental health practice. He and Ron own a small bed and breakfast in Budapest called BudaBaB and Ryan writes a blog named BudgetNomad.

To date, they have visited 61 countries.

"When we left the U.S., everyone thought we were out of our minds and that it would not last. This was back in 2001, long before blogs were well known, so I left with about 50 e-mail addresses of people who wanted regular updates. That list turned into 250 as friends shared with friends who did not want to be second in line for the next missive.

"Ron returns every year for three to four weeks to visit family and friends while I stay here to run the B and B. The last time I was in the U.S. for a vacation was in 2003, but that was before the Supreme Court gave equal rights to same sex couples." (On April 19, 2014 Ryan and Ron were married in Iowa, Ron's home state).

"With the exception of one younger brother, I have no immediate family left. I would rather spend my vacation money on places I have not yet been to rather than jumping around the States to visit friends. I certainly cannot afford to return to the U.S. to live and, at my age, I would never find a significant position worthy of a doctorate degree and more than 25 years of teaching experience. Although I could still do private practice as a therapist, it would take too much time to build a clientele.

"For me, leaving the U.S was less about getting off the treadmill and more about reclaiming my life. I was completely burned out as a social worker and therapist. I didn't enjoy where we were living in California; I desperately needed change.

"Aside from that, there was shrinking economic security in continuing to live in California. At one point I had 22 contracts with various health agencies while also teaching at the junior college. Through attrition or for other business reasons, all the agencies merged or closed completely, threatening my income as I was self-employed. Fear of not having enough work/income and hating where I lived was enough to thrust me forward into the unknown. There was no longer any 'security' at home.

"Moving overseas was like stepping out on faith that things would work out. Ron could be content anywhere and we had his income and our savings to fall back on. The underlying assumption was that we could return to the U.S., find a place on the east coast, and I could work as a therapist if need be or teach as an adjunct instructor. That may or may not have been a valid assumption, but it worked to keep us moving forward while not testing the theory.

"I am a natural born worrier and come from a long line of them. When we set out, I had made up my mind I would live in the moment and not plan for tomorrow. This was the toughest thing I ever had to learn. Once we were out of the country, we focused on the here and now."

As a result of his experiences, Ryan started a coaching consulting company called Renovation of a Life where, through e-mail correspondence and Skype calls, he coaches people around the world who want to make changes in their lives. He resigned from teaching at the end of the 2013–2014 semester and is focusing more on his freelance writing.

Ryan and Ron are now embarking on exchanging their home and homesitting for others around the world.

Talon Windwalker was 42 when he made his decision to hit the road in 2011 with his adopted son, Tigger (then nine). The original plan had been to take a three-week trip to Africa but plans continued to evolve until they turned it into a trip without an ending.

So far, the pair has spent time on six continents. Talon has created several Facebook groups, including one called Families On The Move designed for people like him who have picked up their lives and children and journeyed to other parts of the world. The group has more than 250 members and is populated with questions from parents who want to know the best places to visit with kids in India, the easiest way to get from Ecuador to Peru by train, how to find books on home-schooling, or are seeking basic support in travelling, experiencing and learning how other like-minded families make it work.

After meeting and talking extensively with families who were traveling with kids, Talon decided the nomadic lifestyle could work for them so they set out, hand in hand, on their great adventure together.

"Tigger was at the perfect age for travel; old enough to remember experiences and do a variety of things yet young enough to enjoy discovery. I had long ago decided my family and personal motto was 'Live Without Regret.' In that spirit, I decided there was no better time than the present to make my dream a reality."

Having worked as a hospice chaplain in Colorado, Talon was used to seeing people die without fulfilling their dreams. His work skills were highly portable: Medical transcription (which he continued for the first year-and-a-half), travel writing and photography. He wrote and published two books on the road, became a scuba instructor when he lived in Honduras and writes a regular blog (1dad1kid.com) which provides his main source of income.

As for Tigger's education, Talon follows an 'unschooling approach' which is child-directed education.

"Tigger is being educated by the world. He is learning about history, economics, science and math by experiencing them first hand. He practices math when we're grocery shopping and needs to do currency conversions. Rather than just reading about historical events, he goes to the countries where they happened and sees the monuments and buildings.

"Mostly I give him space to pursue topics that interest him. While we're traveling, we have a *lot* of teaching moments. He isn't so interested in writing and math so a lot of it is done through games and we do a lot of informal teaching throughout the day. Travel really helps with this. For instance when we were planning on going to Cuba we had to discuss a lot about U.S. and world history, political science, social studies, and so on. He retains more when he's active, and comprehends better, too, so we do informal lessons while being active as well.

"In school, Tigger had significant issues with anxiety. He had to be medicated to make it through normal days. After four years on the road, he's extremely functional, far more independent, less anxious, more carefree, more social, and has a much broader level of acceptance of others and we have been able to spend serious quality time together. He became a junior open water diver and so far has logged 35 dives. He is preparing for his junior advanced open water certification—something we would never have been able to afford back home. He has become a confident, adventurous and independent person. It's been amazing to watch his transformation.

"As part of 'living without regret,' I wanted to be able to get more *living* into my life. Being a single parent, I wanted to have more time with my child instead of sending him to school and then daycare and having only a few hours a day with him during the week. In the States I would need to work a full-time job (sometimes more) to make ends meet and to be able to enjoy simple things like going camping for spring break or taking an out-of-state trip in the summer. However, in many countries I'm able to work less than half of my previous hours and have a higher quality of life. Because I work from home and home-school my son, we're together virtually 24 hours a day. That's a tremendous amount of quality time together."

Since leaving the U.S., Talon and Tigger have visited more than 27 countries. As Tigger approached the age of 14, the pair was looking into settling down and doing shorter, less frequent trips. At the time of this writing, they were living in Romania where they planned to stay for a while.

"Long-term, I don't really see much changing in our lifestyle," said Talon. "Our longest time spent anywhere so far was eight months on a tiny Caribbean island in Honduras. I think at some point we'll probably pick a place to use as a home base and take shorter trips from there. As a teenager, my son may want to set some roots down for a while, but then again, having grown up in a nomadic lifestyle, he may not. We don't really do a lot of planning. I prefer to let things unfold and pursue ideas when they arise.

"We left the U.S. with $900 in the bank. At first, I thought I needed much more money than is actually required to travel. We've been full-time nomads since May 2011, and we live off less than a quarter of the income I had previously. I'd say our quality of life is 3,000 times better. It's such a wonderful experience to wake up and think: *I know! Let's go to Spain!*" or *"Why don't we go to Cuba next week?"* and then do it. This is true freedom.

"I suffered with chronic depression most of my life, but since I began this nomadic lifestyle I'm joyous and love my life. I'm excited every day because there's always something new to experience."

Jim Trick is a 44-year-old performing songwriter, speaker and life coach who found a way to transform his life—without leaving the U.S.

In May, 2014, he took leave from his job as an optician in Massachusetts and, together with his wife, Alison, set off on a three month "epic adventure." On the week of his return, his blog read:

> The moment when you realize your dream is
> better than you dreamed, so much so that you
> begin to fear the sleep that many see as normal life.
> What's next?
> More…
> and more and more…
> Adventure, inspiration, transformation…
> To those of you who came along via Facebook,
> thanks so much!
> We are just getting started!

Jim and Alison traveled 10,500 miles throughout the U.S. and, along the way, realized they would never return to their old lifestyles.

"I left my job so I could pursue what was in my heart," said Jim. "With regard to finances, I decided I would hemorrhage money during this trip and be OK with it. I decided if the whole thing went bust that trying would have been the only reward I needed. We packed the car and went."

Jim's focus is now on inspiring and sharing his experiences with others who may be "stuck." While he is based in Massachusetts working part time as an optician, he travels constantly to speak at conferences and produces events designed to inspire and encourage people to pursue their dreams.

"My inspiration for change was centered around the desire for impact. When I used to talk about frustrations that seemed to keep me stuck, people would say 'you have to find your motivation.' I'd contemplate that advice over and over but was limiting myself as to what I thought my motivation(s) should be: health, perception, relationships and so on; none of the things on the usual list of motivators resonated with me in a meaningful way.

"In the end it was a friend confronting me about my weight who connected that dot with my personal and professional life. I realized I would never have the impact I desired if I stayed in a morbidly obese body and a job that, while it was well paying and easy, did not engage my heart.

"My process was centered around deciding, in detail, what I wanted. I identified feelings that were at odds with that goal and why I wanted to achieve it. When I acknowledged those feelings, I began to win.

"The other part for me is spiritual. Deep in my heart I had been feeling God was telling me to leap and that the net would appear. We'd seen countless friends and friends of friends get ill and have tragic things happen. 'How long will you wait to leap?' was a question that burned in my heart and I answered by saying 'not another minute.'

"I've learned there's no substitution for commitment and hard work and that when one applies those components with the burning call of one's heart they become unstoppable. **You don't turn one corner one time and arrive.** The other pleasant surprise for me was that the life I originally thought would be amazing is turning out to be a thousand times better than I had imagined."

17
Midlife and the World is My Oyster

*E*llen Bartling left the U.S. at the age of 34 with her husband when he was offered a work opportunity in Prague. Seventeen years later, as a 51-year-old divorced woman, she made a decision to join the U.S. Foreign Service.

Her first post was in Phnom Penh, Cambodia, where she spent two years before taking a post in Uganda, working as an Office Management Specialist at the U.S. Department of State International Affairs.

"I've always had a thirst for adventure, so when I got divorced after living in Prague for 13 years, I chose to remain in the place that had become home, among friends and the social and cultural network I had developed. I continued to pursue career opportunities, which resulted in my following a lifelong desire to apply for a State Department job. I was thrilled to be accepted. In Prague, I did a variety of things when I was married, including serving on a charity committee for an international women's organization and planning fundraisers, teaching English to business people, and editing for Radio Free Europe/Radio Liberty. During my university years, I'd studied foreign languages and lived abroad for a semester then I got a job as a manager in a travel agency to satisfy my desire to explore the world.

"When my husband and I moved overseas, the reaction from friends and family was mixed. Half the people at the travel agency thought I was nuts and half of them thought it would be a great adventure. I suppose they were all right. I remember my mother saying, 'Thank goodness your father is not still alive. He'd be worried sick all the time.'

"One of the most surprising things for me was the people who kept in touch. At the time, there was no email or Internet so my friends and family had to rely on airmail letters. Some people I thought would stay in touch didn't and others I hadn't expected to stay in touch did—and they remain email or Facebook friends to this day. Another surprising attitude came after my divorce. I'd lived abroad for 13 years by that time and was surprised that a few old friends (mostly those who had never left my home state), my uncle and a few other people actually expected me to move back home, to a state I hadn't lived in since the age of 23 (more than 20 years prior). Instead, I chose to remain abroad in a place that had become home.

"After the divorce, my standard of living dropped, especially because most of my work was freelance and the divorce laws weren't as equitable as in the U.S. Now that I'm in the Foreign Service, I'm pretty low on the totem pole but it's work I love and there are a lot of benefits. Housing is part of the package, I get to live abroad, meet and work with interesting people and the income is steady."

According to the U.S. Department of State website, more than 5,000 people apply each year to join the Foreign Service which is open to anyone between the ages of 20 and 59. There are approximately 15,000 U.S. Foreign Service Officers serving in more than 165 countries.

Susan Spencer was a successful marketing communications (marcom) executive in San Francisco who lived comfortably in a trendy neighborhood and took short trips during her free time. At the age of 50 she made the decision to change the direction of her life.

"During my business career I read and dreamed about traveling abroad but didn't do it. I longed to work overseas but had no angle or advantage—language skills, business specialty or ethnic background—to make me an attractive candidate for any job or project abroad and I needed to keep working to support myself, wherever I was living.

"I was tired of business and of working terribly hard to make rich people richer. I had never identified with the mentality of working your way up the ladder to money and power and being consumed by consumer capitalism.

"Around 2002, the dot-com bubble burst. Companies were downsizing, reorganizing and reshuffling and hiring 20-somethings on the cheap in PR and marcom—and I just couldn't see myself there anymore."

In 2002 she decided to make a radical change, one that took her back to university in early 2003 to complete a master's degree in teaching with the intent of becoming an English teacher abroad. She was accepted at the University of San Francisco so was able to live at home and continue to make money consulting while she was studying.

"Reaction to my going back to school was varied. Friends and business associates mostly thought: *Are you crazy to do this after 50? To go back to being a student in a class of 20 and 30-somethings?* Most had pedestrian ideas that I should use my experience to develop another business or upgrade my skills. They thought I was crazy to pay tuition to yet another university (I already had two college degrees—a bachelor's and a master's—and had worked on a PhD).

"Others, probably with a little poorly masked envy, said 'Wow, that's great,' and then (unhelpfully) added, 'I wish I could do that but I have (fill in the blanks) kids, a responsible job, a husband….' So I just did it and stopped talking about it."

Susan's first assignment was to Guangdong, China where she taught at Shantou University for two years, earning less than she had in the U.S. but with a steady income, a far lower cost of living and housing provided by the university. She describes herself as "never happier." From Guangdong, she went to Beijing where she taught for a further two years, then went back to the U.S. as her father was having health problems.

"I tried to adjust to living and working in the U.S. again but the call to go abroad was too strong. I applied for the State Department English Language Fellow program and accepted an assignment after my father died."

Susan again moved overseas—this time to Turkey where she taught English for three years—until family obligations forced her to move back to the U.S. once again.

"For years, lots of books (travel, fiction based in other countries) had influenced me but it was really the overwhelming feeling of being trapped in an unhappy life where I didn't fit that made me make a change. Perhaps, like so many other expats, I wanted a chance to start fresh and not be surrounded by people who knew the old me and constantly reminded me of it. I needed to escape from a trap of my own making."

While there were challenges in living abroad as a single woman, Susan discovered the advantages outweighed the disadvantages. "The disadvantages were due to my limitations only, and the more I overcame my limitations, the better each day became.

"Work has always been important to me. To be able to live and work in another culture where you have something valuable to contribute and are appreciated (and well-compensated) for it is a great feeling.

"Being an outsider and a foreigner was a positive experience. My life was purposeful and I had something valuable to contribute. For better or worse, I've always been a person who has needed to feel appreciated, and I found that in my situations in China and Turkey. I could also do things as an English teacher overseas that I could never have done in the U.S.

"I was able to do better working overseas at good but not high-paying jobs, than I would have scrambling for low-paying jobs in the U.S., assuming I could even have obtained them in the current job market. I was fortunate to have good situations abroad which, while not high-paying like some of the corporate jobs people salivate over, were adequate for living comfortably but not extravagantly. The jobs paid for annual round-trip airfare, housing and some of my living allowances and amenities and allowed me to have money for travel while working abroad. I found I could live abroad more comfortably than I had in the

U.S. and with a steady income so I didn't have to worry about money all the time, as I did in the States.

"For example, at Shantou University in Guangdong Province, I achieved some notoriety as a public speaking coach; at Beijing Foreign Studies University I became a private English tutor to a very high-ranking official in the Chinese Communist Party; at Ondokuz Mayis University I worked closely with the Turkish Ministry of Education at the highest levels of university leadership, and on and on.

"There's no way I would have had the credentials or competitive horsepower to have any such opportunities in the U.S. In the States, I struggle to cobble together part-time teaching jobs in a market flooded with English teachers who are a lot more ambitious about promoting themselves than I ever could be."

After spending three years in Turkey, Susan was required to return home to care for an ailing mother who later passed away. She's now living in the U.S. while she takes care of selling her family home and she craves the freedom of heading back overseas. "Life has been more challenging for me since returning to the U.S. It's been a little over a year since my mother's death and it has been a difficult period; one in which I first became acquainted with the depression that the writer Andrew Solomon describes as 'not the opposite of happiness, but of vitality.' I've become acutely aware of how much the lack of purposeful engagement and the lack of community can eat away at vitality.

"Maybe it is merely that living in a foreign country provides constant sensory input and experiences that I don't find here, or perhaps I am romanticizing the past (as I do remember exasperating incidents and frustrating times) but there's an emptiness here that I can't seem to fill. I've often tried to express it to people who can't understand wanting to live in a foreign country *(Isn't it hard? Isn't it lonely? Don't you miss things here?)* that living in another culture, trying to make your way using another language, getting by in a system you don't really understand, puts you off balance in a good way; it keeps you on edge, like when you are skiing or skating, or sailing and a gust of wind fills the sail in just the right way.

"Living in another country helps you realize how wrong you were about all the things you were so sure about. It changes our minds, changes our perspectives and priorities. It is humbling and energizing at the same time. It can be inspiring and frustrating, but it is always just plain interesting. You have to accept that you are going to make a lot of mistakes (only in retrospect are they mistakes) and bad decisions (ditto) and probably get scammed and scared and be uncomfortable a good part of the time, but your life will change and you will change and somehow that will give you a sense of peace and satisfaction that you couldn't get through all your other strivings.

"Traveling, of course, was way up there on the list of delights in this new life. My jobs compensated me well enough so I could travel whenever there was a break—and that had been one of my priorities when deciding to move abroad. While living in China, I was able to visit Tibet. While living in Turkey, I went to Egypt twice. I traveled a lot 'in country' and had some unforgettably wonderful experiences.

"Also, making friends, real friends, was way up there on the scale of foreign delights. I have many students who I have lost touch with, of course, but also several who I have seen go on to start families, pursue graduate studies, rise through the job ranks, catch the travel bug and visit exotic places. I made friends with my teaching colleagues, got to know their families, sometimes traveled with them, helped their children with English at times—and most of all, *laughed!* Why was it so easy to laugh together with foreign friends, sometimes laughing together when I wasn't even sure if everyone was even laughing about the same thing—or laughing at my expense— and it didn't matter? The friendships were an essential part of the experience, and without them there would have been an emptiness. I feel far more isolated in the United States—where friends are few and far between—than I ever felt living and working abroad.

"And of course, you get to reinvent yourself! People laugh at this, but there's something very liberating about leaving behind bad situations and the voices in your head that constantly go off when you are reminded of them. There's a certain idea that you can never really get away from yourself, never really change, but I think that a lot of who we are can be situational. By changing our situations we can get a boost to change ourselves. At least that happened to me."

John Pike, another 50-something professional, signed up with the British organization VSO International (Voluntary Service Overseas) at the age of 53, after working for more than 20 years as an investment banker/economist of an international bank and as a barrister in London.

He travelled to Phnom Penh in 2009 where he worked as a volunteer for a Cambodian NGO, using his skills in finance and law to help poor farmers. He negotiated aid contracts with major funders such as USAID and the EU, worked on improving microfinance and credit union development, provided training on fraud investigation and corruption for government officials, and provided education for tribal people on such things as indigenous land rights and tactics to fight land grabbing.

"I didn't feel it was a big change, just another adventure. I had decided long ago that money and power were not especially interesting in themselves so I'd already made several career changes. I wanted an opportunity to live life in high definition in an exotic, less developed country, having previously experienced how enjoyable this was living in Japan for five years and was keen on having another challenge.

"There was a glass ceiling on my second career as a barrister because of age discrimination and, while I loved the job, I wanted to bank the enjoyment and take my skills elsewhere where I could pay back something to society.

"Up to that point, my life had been totally focused on my three daughters, so I thought it would be healthy to break out once they were grown and on their way while my health was still good."

In Phnom Penh, John lived in a two-bedroom apartment that costs $320 per month and estimates his annual costs amount to around $15,000.

"I know now that I can live in poverty perfectly well, having done so for several months in Kampong Cham (a small Cambodian town). I have experienced personal satisfaction from finding money and designing projects for tribal people and from being allowed into their lives and sharing food and bantering with them, if only to a limited extent.

"Material things have even less appeal though I was going in that direction anyway. Interesting experiences and people are much more satisfying."

For **Ginny Anderson**, 59, a prolonged illness in her 30s and a three-month trip to Asia in her 50s was inspiration for her to make a right-angle turn in her life.

"A major influence for changing my life was that I had been ill and mostly bed/housebound for ten years when I was 38. **I knew how quickly everything important can change and how your future hopes and dreams can vanish.**

"It took me years to return to a normal life, slowly returning to work over a period of three years, from two hours a week to part-time to full-time. I was so thrilled to be back 'doing' but it took another five years to realize that the enormous time and effort spent becoming well again was being lost into work. Surely I hadn't gone through such a horrendous physical and emotional journey to end up overworking and getting stressed? What about the new relationship I was in that wasn't getting enough attention because I was travelling for work too much? What about time for me? Hadn't I learnt any lessons?

"I'd get home late, tired and stressed, a meal waiting for me, a bath then bed. This didn't seem to be the work-life balance my job in healthcare management was promoting. I felt I had to seize the opportunity to travel and explore a bit more while I was well enough to do so."

In 2008, Ginny and her partner, Andrew, made the decision to travel from their home in London to experience Asia.

"I had become increasingly dissatisfied and stressed at work, spending too much time on computers and in meetings, and felt that it was time for something different.

"My partner and I discussed the possibility of living abroad and travelling, living on our savings. We turned in our resignations, found someone to live in our flat and look after my cat, and went off for an initial six months. We spent a further two years off and on travelling in Asia and by accident settled in Nha Trang, Vietnam because I had a prolapsed disc in my back and had to stay for six weeks in one place. After the six weeks had passed, we realized we'd started feeling like locals. The hawkers recognized us and stopped hassling us to buy, we knew the good places to eat, and accommodation and the cost of living were fairly cheap. It was good to stop travelling, unpack the rucksack and feel at home. Five years later we're still here."

Since Ginny and Andrew are not retired, they don't receive pensions so they are living off their savings, but they find the cost of living in Vietnam is low enough so they don't have to cut back on anything. They budget approximately $1,000 a month which includes an annual trip to the UK and a holiday somewhere in Asia. The cost of apartments in Nha Trang is between $400 and $500 per month and dinners out cost around $10 for two (with drinks). When they travel in Vietnam, they spend around $12 per night for hotel rooms and take inexpensive buses or trains.

They are able to find good private hospitals in the major cities and have medical insurance that covers emergencies. A recent trip to a dentist for a root canal and a new crown cost $40. "We were both savers so we had enough money to live on while we were travelling. It's a bit scary getting your last pay slip and realizing there may not be another one coming for a long time but the cost of living is so much cheaper here that we have a good quality of life. We hadn't planned to stay for as long as we have. However with the current economic situation and the cost of living in the UK, it makes no sense to return.

"A few years ago, I felt incredibly homesick so we went back to live in the UK for four months. I found short-term contract work fairly quickly but after a few weeks, I realized my heart just wasn't in it; I felt disconnected from all that I'd done before. I worked out my contract and we went straight back to Asia."

18
Midlife and Beyond

Gloria Powell celebrated her 61st birthday having high tea at an historic Spanish mansion in Cuenca, Ecuador, where she moved in 2013.

Like other people we interviewed, Gloria was "ready to get out of the corporate rat race but not ready to fully retire," so she changed her circumstances and left her native Rhode Island to begin a new life in a cheaper, easier and more easygoing environment.

She quit her high level job after working more than 25 years as a marketing and communications executive in Providence and bought a one-way ticket to Ecuador, where she'd found a job as an English teacher in Cuenca.

"At that point in my life, I was not ready to fully retire," she said. "I also needed to allow for a window of time before I could start pulling down Social Security but still live comfortably, safely, and have high quality healthcare. Ecuador met all those needs."

By traveling to Ecuador on a cultural exchange visa (sponsored through the school where she teaches), Gloria was able to relocate without risk or having to pay the upfront costs required for a residency visa, giving her time to decide if she wanted permanent residency status. She found the job during a two-week trip in 2012 when she visited and interviewed at several schools in Quito, Guayaquil, and Cuenca. Preferring the lifestyle of a smaller city, she pursued the director of a school in Cuenca and was accepted six weeks later.

"The climate is wonderful here in the Andes—no humidity, 65–85 degrees year round, and a relatively low cost of living. Cuenca is safer than Providence in terms of crime and outside of the downtown area, the air is clean. Healthcare and prescription drugs are considerably less expensive than in the U.S. and most expats over 60 pay $800–$1,500 a year for a full medical insurance policy so I have most of my prescriptions covered— not bad for someone over 60.

"I love not having a car and all the costs associated with it. I walk at least an hour a day and take a $2 taxi ride at night or whenever I need one. Like most expats here, I've dropped some weight and feel fitter than I have in a long time.

"I don't see myself teaching English long-term, but I'm enjoying it for a year or two. It's been a wonderful way to develop local Ecuadorian friendships as many of my students are adult professionals. I also receive free Spanish and salsa dance lessons, and that has been very helpful in learning a language I've never studied before. Although I do miss seeing my family at times, I have no regrets and plan on spending about six weeks every year in the U.S. My family and friends come to visit often, and Ecuador is a great locale to travel from to other nearby South American countries.

"One of the most interesting things for me has been an expanded view of the world. And thousands of U.S. citizens have made a similar choice. The world gets much smaller when you're an expat and, after only a year living overseas, I now have good friendships with folks based out of Europe, Australia, Turkey, Thailand, and all over the U.S. In many ways, life is simpler and more fulfilling without all the distractions of American life and consumerism."

JUST GO! LEAVE THE TREADMILL FOR A WORLD OF ADVENTURE

—240—

19
Just the Two of Us

Travelling alone has benefits and liabilities. The benefits include independence, lack of responsibility and freedom to decide whatever you want to do and wherever you want to go. Liabilities include loneliness, financial limitation, less personal security and having nobody to share the experiences with. This chapter tells the stories of travelers who've been lucky enough to have the companionship of someone they care about while they figure out where to go and how to spend their lives.

While some couples weren't always in total agreement about timing or specific pursuits, one common denominator always kept them both on the same path: the desire to soak up new experiences and see the world through different eyes.

One couple told us they felt the experience of moving abroad would either bring a partnership closer or drive it farther apart. The following couples experienced the former: **Lauren Tivey** was 41 when she decided to leave the U.S. to teach English abroad. Fortunately, her fiancé, Scotsman **Gerry McGeechan,** was on the same page.

Working in a variety of jobs while she completed her master's degree in English literature in New Hampshire, Lauren convinced Gerry (who worked as an accountant in the U.S.) to travel to Peru and get certified teaching ESL (English as a Second Language).

"Jobs suited to our talents were non-existent in our small town so we started thinking," said Gerry. "Lauren had always wanted to go into the Peace Corps but we thought about teaching English because we could travel the world and get paid for it and have a bit more freedom of choice to choose a location. You can get ESL certified anywhere but Lauren was attracted to Peru. I agreed so we quit our jobs, put our stuff in storage and headed there.

"Both of us have always had the travel bug, and making a life abroad with all the travel perks that accompany it fulfilled life-long goals. Finishing the degree and saving money were steps toward those goals," said Lauren. "There was no *big realization;* we always knew that's what we wanted to do, so we just kept a steady eye on our goal. When the time was right, we left."

After getting their ESL certifications, Lauren and Gerry landed in a Chinese town close to Shanghai.

"Knowing that Asia paid well, we wanted to find a job in China," said Gerry. "When I get to a place I become comfortable and am happy to stay there. With Lauren, though, it's different. She comes up with ideas and places we should visit, and I organize. She takes me out of my comfort zone and it usually turns out to be an amazing adventure. We make things happen and I'm happy to go where she wants—unless it's up a mountain as I'm not a fan of heights."

Lauren is an English literature teacher and Gerry is a world history teacher, both working in the advanced placement program at a high school in Jiangsu Province. When they first arrived in China, however, they were both unprepared for their initial experiences and relieved to have a partner to share them with.

After working with a Chinese ESL placement agency and being accepted into jobs through email and a voice chat interview, they arrived in their host city and discovered it wasn't quite as they'd expected.

"The apartment was horrifying and covered in a layer of years-old grime," said Lauren. "There was litter on the floor and the place stank. There were two tiny bedrooms and no heater and it was freezing inside; you could see your breath in the air. Exposed, frayed wires stuck out of the walls at various places and the toilet was a squatter, just a hole in the floor. It was disgustingly dirty. We were beyond mortified."

Realizing things would not get better, she and Gerry made a hasty escape and landed in Jiangyin, a city of 1.3 million people where they live in a comfortable apartment. For Lauren, who has two daughters in their late 20s and three granddaughters living in the U.S., the biggest sacrifice of living abroad is missing family and not being there for special occasions such as weddings, births, deaths and graduations. "When my seven year old granddaughter asks us over Skype why we can't be there, and when are we coming home, it's kind of heartbreaking. We figure, Well, we just have to fly her over here, and instill the same love of travel, wonderment of the universe, excitement over the different and adventures of an eyes-wide-open life—to bewitch her as we, ourselves, have been bewitched. And when we all meet up for a family gathering in Italy next year, that's exactly what we're going to say to them, our children and grandchildren. We'll regale them with stories, show them treasured mementos, and urge them to **travel, travel, travel, as life is too short to ignore the rest of the big blue planet out there.**"

In exchange for missing family and friends, however, Lauren and Gerry have one another and their common dream of exploring the world. Their teaching positions provide them with a free apartment, lucrative employment with perks, summers off, the benefit of beefing up their CVs and the ability to save money.

"No more drudgery of an hourly wage at some American chain store, no more merely scraping by, paycheck to paycheck, no more car payments, no more inane television chatter, fast food drivethroughs or religious bumper stickers. Now every day is a bona fide adventure, a real magic trick we've somehow pulled off. And it's *addictive,*" said Lauren. "In fact, if it weren't for missing family, we'd probably never want to return to the U.S. Moving abroad completely changed our lives for the better. Don't get us wrong; it's not all wine and roses; there are plenty of daily hurdles to overcome. Certain days can be great: charming and enchanting one moment, then quickly changing to frustrating and challenging the next, on both large and small scales. The particularly difficult experiences have held rewards of their own, as every time we get past one, we find ourselves stronger, more adapted, and proud of ourselves.

"Our limits have been pushed, and we find ourselves to have expanded (mentally, emotionally, physically, and yes, spiritually) and our proverbial horizons broadened. Even when times are darkest, when we're sick of the food, tired of the constant battle to communicate, frustrated with all the mysterious cultural differences, and severely missing our families, we've looked back at our struggle to survive in our home countries, and agreed that the opportunities available to us abroad far outweigh the comforts of home.

"Most important to us, however, is the ability to travel inexpensively to exotic locales—something both of us have dreamed of since childhood. We used to salivate over destinations like Tibet, Burma and Japan, and now we are fortunate enough to be able to visit them all."

Dani and Jess met in a small town in Germany where Jess was teaching English and Dani was enrolled in an international business degree program. They moved to England together in 2006 and, in April 2010, hit the road at the respective ages of 31 and 29 and launched their website, Globetrotter Girls.

"In the middle of a long, gray British winter in January 2010, we decided to break free and fly to Las Vegas on the first leg of what we thought would be a year-long trip around the world," said Jess. "We didn't have much in the way of savings and we had limited experience with long-term travel. I was working as a copywriter/content creator and Dani was a recruitment consultant in the financial sector. We realized that, instead of sitting in our kitchen in London, we could work from anywhere—Guatemala, Rio, Thailand. So we did. Our plan was to take our jobs on the road and see where it all would lead."

With no home base to speak of, Jess and Dani combine months of short trips with longer stays living as locals.

"In England we earned enough to take several smaller inter-Europe trips and one long-distance trip each year," said Jess. "But we never felt satisfied with our limited travel time. Once we cut out rent, bills and any other recurring payments, we lived much more comfortably while we traveled.

"Sometimes we research hotels and hostels like crazy before settling on one. Other times we wing it once we get into town. In cities like Berlin or Buenos Aires, we rented vacation apartments for five or six weeks at a time, and our favorite long-term option is house-sitting which we have done more than 15 times across four continents in the last 3 ½ years.

"The hardest part was that we had been based in a country that was neither of our native countries so our bank accounts, taxes and business bases were foreign to our locations. But the great things about being nomadic include benefiting from low-cost high-quality healthcare around the world and, of course, experiencing dozens of different cultures and ways of life each year. And most important, being both location and financially independent gives us the nerve to actually *dream* and feel in control of our own destinies."

For **Susanna and Mark Perkins**, the lack of work and cost of living in the U.S. were adequate enough reasons for them to move from Florida to Panama in 2012. "We couldn't afford to live in the U.S.," said Susanna, in her late 50s in 2014. "I was not earning enough to match my previous salary, and health considerations made it impossible for me to work the extra hours that would have been needed to make that happen. In March 2009, the company I worked for melted down in the financial mess and a few years earlier I'd been diagnosed with Type 2 diabetes. I simply couldn't work the 60–80 hour weeks I had when I was younger. My husband, who had just received his master's degree, could only find work as a bicycle courier. So we opted for a lower cost, slower pace of life.

"I've always wanted to experience life in another culture, but economic conditions drove our decision. Although travel is something I'd always wanted, I felt very angry for a long time that it had become my only viable choice.

"In the U.S., we were falling deeper into debt every month, couldn't afford to see doctors, and had cut every expense it was possible to cut. Here in Panama we can live with moderate comfort on our income."

When they made the decision to move, the couple didn't receive a great deal of support and they found some of their friends to be less than encouraging.

"Oh, boy, was it a mixed bag! Some friends were furious; others were curious; others—the minority, I'm sad to say— were supportive. My family was reasonably supportive and encouraging and my mother went so far as to admit she was proud of us for being so courageous and forward thinking. Our kids' reactions ranged from, "fantastic" to "well, I understand." "My husband's family didn't give us a lot of support. His sister and brother have an "I don't get it and I don't agree with it but I suppose if it makes you happy it's OK" type of attitude. His mother is furious that we left, and of course blames me completely."

The Perkinses packed up their three dogs and took them to their new Central American home where they rented a house in Las Tablas. Mark is retired and Susanna works full-time in her own online consulting businesses—one of their websites, Future Expats Forum, chronicles their process of moving abroad and the other helps non-technical people learn about building websites.

They have five grown children in the U.S. and visit occasionally but have no desire to move back home.

"I'm hoping to retire (at least semi-retire) in a couple of years, and I really want to enjoy where I live and what I do at that point. Although there's an awful lot we like about Las Tablas, we're not ready to settle down and dig in for the long haul. More exploring is definitely in our future!

"We're fortunate in that we mostly complement each other. If one of us is frustrated or fed up with some aspect of our life here, the other one's okay with it so we help each other along.

The one exception was a couple of months where we both hit the same wall at the same time. We had been in the States for a month-long visit, and returned home to Panama just before Thanksgiving. It was our first set of holidays without any of our kids, and we were completely miserable."

20
And The Family Came Too

*I*t may not seem like a big deal to travel solo or even as a couple. But that's not the only type of traveler who packs a backpack and heads off on journeys to far-flung parts of the world.

Among the most impressive voyagers we came across were those who had one, two or even *five* children in tow. They included couples who felt they weren't getting enough quality time with their kids, parents who wanted to expose their young ones to worlds that would educate them beyond the classroom and single parents who defied their peers and took a time-out from traditional education and after-school activities.

Greg and Rachel Denning fell into the *"you've gotta be kidding me"* category when they started travelling in 2007 with four kids aged four, three, 18 months and three months. They now have six children, including a toddler who was born in Costa Rica in 2014.

Their website, DiscoverShareInspire, opens with the words: *"Hi there! We're the Dennings. We are normal people. Except that we live a ridiculously awesome life."*

There's nothing "normal" about this remarkable family, though. They hit the road after their fourth child was born and drove from the U.S. to Costa Rica where they lived for a year on a good income from stock market and real estate investments. A year later, the stock market crashed, taking a chunk of their savings with it and forcing them back to the U.S. to look for work.

They saved for a year, then headed to the Dominican Republic where their plans didn't go as hoped. They were soon back in the U.S. to recharge their batteries. After six months in the States, they were offered positions with a non-profit organization in India. They leapt at the chance, spent five months in Tamil Nadu then returned to Atlanta to add another child to their family.

At that point, they decided to travel from Alaska to Argentina in a car powered by recycled vegetable oil and, since then, have spent time in Belize, Costa Rica, Nicaragua, Panama, Guatemala, El Salvador and Mexico. By the time he's five years old, their youngest son Atlas will have visited 20 countries.

"In 2007 we decided to sell all our stuff and go *nomad,*" said Rachel. "Our decision was based on a burning desire to *live deliberately*—we wanted to consciously design our family lifestyle to include the things that really mattered to us—travel, adventure, language, culture, fun, education and making a positive impact on the world. Our aim is to live simply, maximize our freedom, and escape the mundane.

"Our greatest challenges have been figuring out how to fund our travels. When we left a 'job' in the U.S., we weren't sure how to earn money any other way. We'd been trained to think income equals job. It's been a process figuring out how to make it work without an employer, but very rewarding as well.

"We usually spend between $60 and $100 a day for the seven of us; sometimes less when we're actually on the road. We keep costs low by living simply. We prepare our own meals and rent inexpensive houses (usually $200–$250/month). On the road, we usually camp (we have a roof top tent and a homemade camper on our truck) and we drive on recycled vegetable oil when we can find it. We eliminate everything we can that's not essential to free up the time and the money to do what we really want to do.

"At first we didn't know how we would cover the whole trip, but we started with savings, and built our business along the way."

The Dennings finance their travel through income from affiliate marketing, freelance writing assignments and building websites. Rachel has written a book: *Living Deliberately: How We Created a Ridiculously Awesome Life* and sells essential oils online. They sometimes perform home repairs and improvements or work in campgrounds in exchange for accommodation, which may be in forests, fields, parking lots or police stations.

"When we arrive in a place, we ask around—at the markets, stores, wherever. If we need to, we stay at a hotel or camp until we find a place but Greg is very friendly and always strikes up conversations with strangers so we usually find places within one or two days."

When it comes to health and medical needs for the family, their philosophy is to "pay for what is, not for what if."

They maintain a program of exercise and good food, and use natural cures for most things, using essential oils when they can. They don't have health insurance, preferring to deal with medical issues with natural cures and remedies whenever possible.

"Since Greg has received emergency medical training (EMT) and once worked on an ambulance, he knows the value of medical care. If someone needs to go to a doctor, they go. If we have to go to the hospital for some emergency, we pay the bill out of our savings, or make payments on it.

"Travel has become one of the defining elements of our life. It is something we do as a family. It's part of who we are. Without travel, our life would lose much of its meaning.

"Travel is how we educate our children. It's how we learn about the world, and how we make a contribution to make it a better place. It's helped us to grow as individuals, and as a family, by bringing us closer together, increasing our confidence, and helping us to have more compassion for others and gratitude for what we have.

"Many people say they can't travel because they have children but I feel the pros outweigh the cons of traveling with kids; you'll never regret doing it. It's not sunshine and roses all the time and there are definitely challenges but being a parent is challenging, no matter where you are. Ultimately, I think you should do it. The memories you'll create together are irreplaceable."

Single mother, **Ruth J**, was 50 and down to her last $20 when she decided she needed a major change in her life.

"I was working a full-time job as a leasing manager for shopping centers, and had my own business at home selling clothes on eBay in Australia," she said. "I would drop my son off at 7a.m. and normally work until midnight. We had no fun, no money and no life. I was moving backward paying off a house. I had no time to enjoy a social life. I had no money and it was horrid.

"I talked to my son who was then five, and together we made the decision to sell nearly all we owned and perform random acts of kindness as we traveled the world. I sold things on eBay and had garage sales and sold nearly everything: our car, mobile home, house and most of my possessions." "While the decision was made pretty fast, it took about 18 months to prepare for the journey.

"As an older mum, I realized if I didn't travel now with my son, he would be too old to want to travel with me once I became financially stable. Right from the start, we made decisions together. We talked through where we wanted to go and how we would do it. We planned and made decisions about what to keep and what to sell. We prepared the house for sale together. We made agendas.

"I talked to his school as soon as I decided and had meetings with them. I kept him home for a few days so we could practice home schooling and we spent each weekend going for hikes, wearing small backpacks and learning what we needed. The first few times we were unprepared, but each time I came back with more of an idea of what we did and didn't need.

"I experienced a lot of knock-backs and received very little support in making this choice. I had one sister who said I deserved the happiness and a few people who thought I wasn't crazy, but not many. Most questioned me—a lot!"

While they were in the process of selling their home, Ruth and her son took on a house-sitting gig for a friend which got them hooked on the concept. After their house sold, they took on another assignment to take care of a neighbor's home so they could clean up their own and hand it over to the new owner.

Once their home sold, they started applying for other house-sitting opportunities. They landed their first in a place many people dream about—an island in Fiji—for six weeks. Ruth's son attended a local school there until Ruth decided to home school him. Then she discovered world schooling (where travel and experiences act as the classroom) which she is now using. To supplement their house-sitting assignments, they couch surf or stay in small hotels or hostels.

"We travel fairly fast given the fact most countries only allow you a three-month visa. Being a single mum on a budget can get tiring and expensive. Hotels can get lonely, and hostels can be dirty, so house-sitting gives us the time to slow down, for my son to catch up on his learning, and for both of us to make new friends among the locals.

"Make no mistake; there are tough times traveling. The hardest thing by far is budgeting. The second as a single parent is making wise decisions on my own without being able to talk them over with anyone. This journey has made me more patient and, at the same time, I love offering random acts of kindness and I long to do little things to change the world. The more I give as we travel, the more I want to do.

"If I had time over again, I would invest or do something to make my money last longer. I would give more, travel with less, and probably not spend so long blogging. I would hug more strangers, and I would try more foreign foods. This journey costs pretty much the same as living at home and every day we are thankful and draw closer to one another. I hope one day I can write a book, talk to single mums, or enlighten anyone I meet that there is more to life than paying off a house, working till the wee hours of the morning, and not following your dream."

Anthony Watanabe and his wife, **Rosariet (Rose) Swagemakers** had the same desire for their children when they approached their Canadian school and explained they'd be taking their two young sons, Emile and Felix (aged 10 and 8) out of class for a year. The school was in full support.

"Nothing 'dramatic' moved us toward travelling the world for a year, only inspiration," said Rose. "We call this trip our 'mid-life inspiration' rather than our mid-life crisis. We want more and better connection time as a family and a year to step back to evaluate our current business and explore new business opportunities both at home and abroad.

"We originally had the goal to leave in 2017, but when close friends starting getting ill around us, we read the book, *The*

4-hour Work Week and loved the idea of taking mini sabbaticals during our lifetime. Then some unexpected business changes arose and we realized that now was the best time for us. Our children still want to be with us, and we are still young and fit enough to travel (and sleep in hostels around the world). This is an opportune time to set the basis for a 'world education' that will hopefully shape the children's paths from here on.

"Our greatest challenge has been homeschooling our children. Finding a routine is not always easy when you move around so we have had the best results when we stayed in one location for 3–4 weeks. We have learned along the way (and are still learning) what motivates our children—such as online, interactive math programs, variety in what they are learning and enrolling them into local programs such as art and music."

Since Rose and Anthony are both trilingual (English, Dutch and French), they are raising their sons to speak several languages—often with Ruth speaking English to them and Anthony speaking French. They educate them on the road by giving them assignments based on the countries they visit—such as the project they had to complete about Cambodia before they arrived in the country so they could learn about its history and culture.

"Our greatest delight has been seeing our children develop into confident young men who enjoy sharing their travel experiences with adults and children of varied nationalities and backgrounds. They are sponges that absorb each new experience with such intensity and joy and it is fantastic to watch."

Anthon, Rose and their sons are living in Bangkok where Anthony has started a small business and the boys are in school.

Another family with a unique lifestyle is the **Bohemian Travelers family,** consisting of Mary and Jeff and their three sons, Dylan, Colin, and Theo.

They moved from the U.S. to Costa Rica in 2006 with two boys (aged seven and three), had another child and lived there for five years, then decided to embark on a life of constant travel to "get out of our comfort zone."

"Before we left the U.S., we were living the 'American dream'— in debt and working our butts off to stay above water," said Mary. "We had a huge house with all the toys you could want. I worked as a registered nurse and my husband had two jobs: a real estate business and a day job working for a beer distributor, so we could have healthcare.

"We left for a lot of reasons. It hit us that we'd be living this life for years just trying to hang on to things. What would that be teaching and showing our children? We knew we'd never truly own anything, and paying a fortune for the next 30 years seemed insane. That, coupled with the political environment in the U.S. back then and the fact that we wanted the kids to know the difference between what they need and what they want, helped us make the jump."

When Mary and Jeff moved to Costa Rica they had no home, no car, spoke no Spanish and had no jobs. Jeff started working at a real estate company and made enough money to cover their living expenses. Then their blog took off and started to generate enough income to live on. They had another baby in 2008 and, four years later, decided to leave Costa Rica and start a nomadic lifestyle.

"Interestingly, it all started with a drunken silly conversation about 'what ifs' with some friends back home," said Mary. "They are still at home doing the same-ole-same-ole, but we took that conversation and ran with it! Over the years we've realized that we are the makers of our destiny; we choose to make our dreams come true to show our kids first-hand that the world is theirs and *all* of it is available to them.

"Since leaving the U.S., life has become so much cheaper; it's astonishing. We had been spending $10-15K per month in the U.S. In Costa Rica we're spending closer to $2,000 per month. When we started to think of traveling we decided to start another blog, my travel blog. It started as a way to keep everyone informed and to journal our adventures but it turned into an income stream. We work long hours to keep the blogs running—far more than anyone realizes—but it's worth it to enjoy the freedom and travel that we do."

While travelling with three children has challenges, Mary and Jeff feel the experience of travel has brought them all closer.

"It's slightly difficult at times for my 13-year-old as he misses his friends from the U.S. and Costa Rica, but we have made some adjustments, found some great new traveling online friends, and got him involved in things where we can," said Mary. "We talk with the kids a lot about this lifestyle and gauge how they are feeling. At the moment they say they wouldn't change a thing. It amazes me how pliable they are, and oftentimes they handle the tougher aspects of travel better than we do.

"My message to other people considering a change is a simple one: Take one step today, right now, toward your goal. Do something toward your goal now: a phone call, a little research, chatting with your husband, booking flights, whatever it is to set the ball rolling. We are not exceptional people for doing this, nor are we lucky. We worked hard to accomplish our goal and sacrificed to make it happen. But all it takes to live the life you want is to make the decision to do it."

The Millers are at the extreme end of families living well outside traditional boundaries. Headed by Jenn and Tony, they took off from the U.S. in 2008 with four kids aged five to 11 to bicycle from England to Tunisia and back. Along the way, when they were camped out on a sea cliff on the Adriatic coast of Italy, the stock market crashed. Most of their money vanished.

"At the time, it was frightening and horrible; we were fighting the urge to *freak out,*" said Jenn. "But, in retrospect, it was the best thing that could have happened to us. It pulled the rug out from under us and made us figure out how to take this journey from a 'gap year on savings' to a self-funded lifestyle."

Tony had left a good job with a major computer company so he taught himself new programming languages and began to work freelance. The family headed to Africa, lived cheaply and Jenn began to develop her freelance writing business.

"We saw how fast our kids were growing and wanted to do some really special things as a family that would make great memories but also equip them to live in the world in a way that spending their childhoods in one place within the four walls of a classroom could not," said Jenn. "We travel specifically because of the intersection of education and adventure. We took off when and how we did and continue to travel because we want our children to learn. There are a lot of ways to educate a child and introduce him to the world; one way is to just let the child slowly walk through it for a while and watch the people." Since leaving home eight years ago, the Millers have spent time in 27 countries (most for at least a month).

"One of the big misconceptions people have about our life is that it is somehow magically perfect and we live on perpetual holiday. The truth is that trading a stationary life for a nomadic one often means discomfort, hardship and difficulty. The same worries and struggles travel with you, but they must be dealt with in your third or fourth language and in a culture that is unfamiliar. Our personal struggles, relationship difficulties and parenting processes don't magically evaporate because we happen to have a beach in the background. In fact, those hardships are often compounded by the challenges that travel presents.

"But lifestyle travel has taught us a lot of important lessons. It's bonded our family and our kids in a way that little else could have. **We've learned that very little is out of our reach and there's very little we cannot do if we try.** The children have learned to do hard things—genuinely hard things, not contrived hard things as are so often provided for children—like pushing bikes up mountains and carrying heavy loads for miles on their backs. We've learned that no matter how big a dream is, it can almost always be accomplished if you put your mind to it. The greatest hurdles we face are almost always within ourselves. It's very rarely about money or relationships or physical ability or disability or a job or education. It's really about what goes on inside our own heads. If we can change our thinking, we can change the whole world, or at least the one we live in.

"We aren't guaranteed much in this life; the one breath we are living in is all we have and it is heartbreaking to see people with beautiful dreams waste their existence and sell themselves short of their potential. We can't have it all, and to choose one life means to actively not choose another. For us, the memories and the relationships are what matter. We do without a lot of things so we can have what matters to us. My dad once told me that life is like a coin; you can spend it any way you choose, but you can only spend it once. That's perhaps the best lesson to relearn every single day, because life happens in every breath and we're constantly spending it."

Among other remarkable families we encountered were the **Chentnik family** who moved to China in their 20s with two kids, the **King family** who sold all their possessions and moved to Costa Rica in their 30s with an infant son and a daughter on the way and the **Sathre-Vogel family** who cycled from Argentina to Alaska with their two sons and are now living back in the U.S. after 28 years of travel.

Paz and Ezekiel (Zeek) Chentnik moved to China with their two toddlers where they lived for a year, fell in love with Southeast Asia and spent time in Thailand and Malaysia then headed to South America and Mexico before setting their sights on The Netherlands in 2014. They recently moved to the U.S. for a work assignment and plan on being there for a couple of years before possibly hitting the road again.

Ezekiel was a web engineer for a local company in Milwaukee and Paz worked as district director for the Muscular Dystrophy Association and did business development for one of Microsoft's local partners. After moving from the U.S., Paz taught English after completing a TESOL (Teachers of English to Speakers of Other Languages) certification online. Ezekiel continued to work as a software engineer.

Their idea to leave the U.S. formed in 2009 when they realized their lives were more about working hard and being stressed than enjoying themselves and having time to relax.

"We were running around and never together," said Paz. "We were not happy. I was working crazy and so was Zeek. We were eating out and fighting and never home. All those millions of dollars we were trying to make: where were they going? McDonalds!"

"I decided to quit my job and took a position making $20,000 a year less to spend time with the people I love—not just drive around in a car with them. Then we saw a presentation by David Ramsey at Connection Point Church and saw the light. We were prisoners to our possessions."

In April 2010 when their second child was two months old and their daughter was three, they decided they "wanted to go on an adventure." In February 2011, they arrived in China.

"We wanted to use our lives to *live,* not to wait for something to happen. We wanted to surround ourselves with our children and learn with them. Since leaving the States, we have both lost over 35 pounds; we eat now out of enjoyment instead of anxiety. Our children know so much more than they ever would have learned in school and are far ahead of others their same age. The compassion and love for cultures and people we have been able to teach our children is awesome. We wouldn't trade one minute of it (good and bad) for our old life."

Sabina and Keith King moved to Costa Rica when Sabina was eight months pregnant with her second child then lived in Belize and ended up in Bali where they have lived since June 2012.

"Our biggest influence came from a combination of the desire to travel with a complete financial loss," said Sabina. "It was part design and part necessity. We've had several businesses and each one taught us what we did and didn't want as a lifestyle. In 2008, when everything collapsed in the U.S., we lost every investment and real estate asset we had. Talk of visiting Costa Rica for a vacation soon became an extended vacation and then Mr. King suggested we have our baby there. I thought he was crazy, but after a while it started to make sense to me. Everything fell into place so easily; we knew this was the right decision.

"We budgeted $1,500 to $2,000 per month for our needs; enough for a great life in Costa Rica, but not enough for the U.S. In Costa Rica, we were able to rent a house, have a housekeeper a few times a week and do weekly and monthly trips on that budget.

"Here in Bali, we have a full time nanny, a housekeeper, a gardener and a full-time cook which we'd never be able to afford in the U.S. Our lives are richer living here because we can afford so much more. Even though we lost our investments in the global crisis, we were fortunate as we still had a small online business that generated income and kept us going.

"Once we started to get rid of possessions, we found that less stuff leads not only to more money, but also to more time, more security, more power and more focus on the things or experiences you really want out of life. Less really is more— more of the important stuff. **I think one reason people are so stressed is because of the clutter they have, that they need to pay for, maintain and store.** We don't feel like we've sacrificed anything. We've gained so much time and freedom; any frustrations that come up are minuscule compared to the feeling of lightness we have."

Another intrepid adventurer is **Nancy Sathre-Vogel**, a woman who's done it all—first solo, then with her husband and then with kids.

In 2011, she returned to the U.S. after spending 28 years travelling the globe on an adventure that began with a two-year stint in the Peace Corps in Honduras at the age of 24.

Wanderlust hit hard and, since she was a teacher, Nancy discovered the world could be her oyster. She spent three years teaching on a Navajo reservation, one year biking the Indian subcontinent, two years in Albuquerque, two years in Egypt, seven years in Ethiopia, two years in Taiwan and a year in Malaysia (most of it with her husband, John, who was also a teacher). In 2006, the couple moved back to the U.S. for 15 months then headed out again with their two sons to cycle 27,000 miles from Alaska to Argentina.

Here's a snapshot of her travelling lifestyle over the past 30 years:

- 1980s—Budget backpacker all the way. I spent seven months traveling in Central and South America with a grand total of $3,200 in my pocket.
- Early 1990s—My bike touring days were in full swing. My (now) husband and I spent a year biking around Pakistan, India, Nepal, and Bangladesh. Then, as schoolteachers, we had long-ish vacations, which were spent biking in various countries—including Israel, Yemen, Mali, Baja California.
- Late 1990s/early 2000s—We were living the full-fledged expat life. We had a house in Ethiopia, complete with full-time maid and guards. Our schools paid to fly us back to the U.S. every summer. Every Christmas break was spent in a different country.
- Late 2000s—We made the decision to ditch our high-pressure teaching jobs in favor of a simple life on two wheels. By then, our kids were school age, so we took them out of school

and hopped on bikes. We spent one year biking around the U.S. and Mexico, then another three years pedaling from Alaska to Argentina.

"It came down to time. We realized the clock was ticking and our children were growing up. If we didn't take advantage of now to spend with them, we would lose the opportunity. As teachers, we spent more time with other people's kids and not enough with our own—so we quit to create memories with our own boys. "I can't say I knew others who were out gallivanting around the world on bikes with their children—although I found some after we started. I guess it came down to my husband not being afraid to dream big and push for it to happen."

Nancy is now a motivational speaker and writer who has written five books, and whose personal motto is "What Would You Do If You Were Not Afraid?"

21
All The Way Outside the Box

A ll the people we interviewed impressed us with their spirit of adventure, their desire to do things differently and their intrepid outlook on living their lives outside the proverbial box. Then we met **Ramon Stoppelenburg** who didn't just live outside the box; he didn't even acknowledge there *was* a box. At the age of 24, he decided he'd had enough of working as a journalist in his native Netherlands, and discovered a way he could travel— *without any funds.*

Using his gift for marketing, a talent for blogging and a personality that's hard to resist, Ramon put together a website that became his meal ticket for the next 26 months. Through LetMeStayForADay.com, he tapped into the desire of individuals to host, provide and entertain him in countries around the world. In exchange, he wrote about them and his experiences on his blog. It sounds crazy but it worked. Long before Couchsurfing became a formal entity in 2003, Ramon found his way into homes, beds, trains and planes around the world, thanks to the kindness of strangers. He travelled throughout 18 countries, met approximately 10,000 people and slept in 500 different beds, depending entirely on individuals and corporate sponsors to pay his way. A woman from Calgary sponsored him on a free flight from Amsterdam to Vancouver with her frequent flyer miles. Canadian railway companies provided him with coast to coast travel and a South African travel website sponsored him on a flight to Johannesburg. He started off with 700 invitations from 64 countries and, by the end of the trip, had received 4,000 invitations from 72 countries and more than a million hits on his website each month.

U.S. television networks followed the "notorious Dutch freeloader who travelled the world" and Ramon became a mini-celebrity through his adventurous lifestyle. He followed up his voyage by writing a book about his travels—*Let Me Stay For A Day: Around the World for Free,* studying massage therapy, launching a company that gives tours on Mount Kilimanjaro and hosting European cooking trips. When he landed in Phnom Penh in 2010, he discovered the local movie house, The Flicks, was up for sale. Ramon wanted to run a movie house, but he had no money. So he was off again—launching a website that asked people to lend him funds with a guarantee he'd pay them back within six months. He paid back every dollar and subsequently opened two more locations.

"If there is one disease in my body, it's the urge to go out and explore, enjoy, taste and feel everything that is different from *normal life,*" he said.

"I took off on a journey that made me happy. And without realizing it, I became a guy with an eight hour workweek."

While Ramon puts much more than eight hours into building, creating and marketing his businesses, the beauty lies in the fact that he doesn't consider it work.

He also likes to give back. Not only is he a very active Couchsurfing host (he's nicknamed "The Godfather of Couch Surfing"), he puts a great deal of energy reaching out into his local community (he once invited Cambodian popcorn vendors in Phnom Penh to sell their product at an outdoor film screening so they culd make a generous profit) and he welcomes volunteers to his movie houses in exchange for free board and lodging.

"When people ask me *why* I moved, I always tell them I'm an *economic refugee.* I was tired of having to make a living in the Netherlands, working 45 hours a week as a freelancer, paying almost 50 percent income tax and not having much left at the end of each month. My move to Cambodia brought a major change to my life and a very necessary one. Instead of making a living, I now *thrive.* Most of what I do is fun. If I don't like doing something, I shouldn't be doing it."

Dozens of people have decided to hoist the proverbial anchor, plunge headfirst into unknown adventures and fill their backpacks with trust, dreams and an extra roll of toilet paper. It may not be your life—and it wasn't ours until four years ago—but it's obvious there's a network far larger than we ever imagined of folks who've bypassed the traditional eight-hour workday and figured out a new way to embrace the world.

The other thing we discovered is that all of them are happy and willing to share their experiences, advice and assistance with anyone considering making a life-altering move. Check out their websites and be inspired.

Whether it's taking a TEFL class, volunteering your services for a couple of months or taking a gap year at any point of your life, there are dozens of ways you can find out if a lifestyle of travel, freedom and figuring-it-out-along-the-way is for you.

22
What Does it Cost?

Whenever we talk about stepping off the treadmill and voyaging to exotic (or even not so exotic) places, most people usually have one big question: How much does it cost?

Our cost of living in Cambodia was a fraction of what it was in the U.S., yet our quality of life was immeasurably higher. Before leaving home, Skip and I spent a great deal of time thinking it through and estimating how much we'd need to live. Our first year in Phnom Penh cost around $48,000 and included flights to the U.S. and England, countless short excursions throughout Cambodia and into Thailand. We dined out most days of the week and enjoyed dozens of cheap massages while living in a comfortable rental apartment with high-speed Wi-Fi, air conditioning and cable TV. We entertained liberally and used *tuk-tuks* every day to get around the city. Since then, our annual expenses have fluctuated depending on how much and where we've travelled, and what kind of unanticipated expenses have popped up along the way. Some years we tapped into supplemental funds such as the consulting fees that gave us more disposable income. More recently, we've spent time house-sitting, which has allowed us to spend more on travel and less on fixed costs like lodging.

People we interviewed along the way had their own ways of living and budgeting. Some chose to house-sit to save on costs, some stayed with locals and some chose to eat in cheap neighborhood cafés or cook at home. Others splurged on nice hotels or exotic trips during their voyages. Here's a sampling of what it cost:

Adam Pervez: 30 months (918 days) on the road cost me about $20,000. I kept track of accommodation costs for the entire journey and they totaled $897. My point in traveling was to connect with locals as much as possible, including staying with complete strangers almost everywhere I went so my lodging costs were very low.

I did a bit of a monthly budget for Costa Rica when I traveled there in May, 2012 (a country I found more expensive than the other Central American countries I visited).

During my three weeks there, I spent a total of $249, which included my $18 bus ticket out of Costa Rica, a $16 round trip San Jose–Quepos ticket and a fancy $5 non-aluminum deodorant. This worked out to $11.85 per day.

With regard to healthcare costs, I had catastrophic health insurance that cost me $300 for six months during my travels, but my out of pocket medical care was negligible, maybe less than $200 for the entire journey.

Talon Windwalker and son, Tigger: When we first began it was around $12,000 per year. I started needing more comfort later so our budget slid up a bit and we spent $14,500 last year. That included everything from lodging to food to travel costs. Most countries are much cheaper to live in than the U.S. so it's pretty easy to live on a small budget.

Early on, we bunked in a lot of hostels and cheap hotels with an occasional couchsurfing stay. Later on, I discovered AirBnB and started doing that more often. And after that, I discovered that house-sitting had great potential. In more recent travels, we use AirBnB and look for local apartments and house-sits.

Anthony Watanabe and Rose Swagemakers and their two sons: Our total was $5,000–$6,000 per month with everything included (storage costs, preparation, etc). We estimated $52 per person per day but this is much higher than what we actually spent. Healthcare/insurance was about $1,500 for the year.

Nancy Sathre-Vogel (with husband and two sons): We spent roughly $2,000 per month. Our daily expenses (food, accommodation, etc.) came in at around $50 per day or $1500 per month. We also allotted an additional $500 for one-off expenses, which could be rebuilding the bikes or taking a trip to the Galapagos or Machu Picchu. We would go many months without spending that $500, then blow thousands in a week.

Many people change their budget in accordance with country—more expensive countries have a higher budget—cheaper countries are budgeted less money—but we didn't approach it that way. We had a set budget and figured out a way to live within that by varying how we lived. In the U.S. and Canada, we camped almost exclusively since hotels were expensive. In cheaper countries, we stayed in hotels and the quality varied quite a bit. In some countries we could get really nice hotels for $30; in other countries that same amount would get us a dump. We did the same with food. When restaurants were cheap, we ate there. When they weren't, we cooked our own meals.

Diana Edelman: In Thailand, the rent for my house was $250 a month, electricity about $30 a month and Internet $25 a month. Food can be as cheap as a few dollars a day, and my gym membership was $300 for a year.

Ginny Anderson (and husband): Our monthly sum for every-thing is less than $1,000 for two people here in Vietnam. This includes rent ($480 a month) cost of renewing visas (approxi-mately $60 for three months), one trip to the UK, housing costs that include utilities, food, all shopping needs, entertainment and socializing. We also have one short holiday somewhere in Asia each year.

We eat in about 4–5 times a week, buy local food, and eat out a few nights a week. We have travel insurance that covers medical, which is around $600 each per year.

Lauren and Gerry: Our total living cost per year, per person, in China is less than $5,000.

We get a free apartment on campus so we pay no rent. The cost of utilities is $25–30 each per month and our phone service is around $30 each per month. We spend somewhere between $250 and $350 a month each for food. We have health insur-ance through our employer which pays 80%. What we make over and above that amount gets banked or goes toward travel.

Ate Hoekstra: My living cost is between $10,000 and $15,000 per year in Cambodia. That includes rent, food, insurance, trans-portation and everything else I need.

Gloria Powell: Living in Cuenca costs me around $1,000 per month, which includes eating out two or three times a week, paying for healthcare (around $70 per month), entertainment and buying groceries. I lease a large house and rent out rooms to other teachers so that it pays for itself, and I walk most places so I don't have a lot of transportation expense.

Ruth J. and son: Our average travel costs are $60 a day not including major flights. I used to have travel /health insurance, but when my son ended up in hospital and the bill came to $11 for two days in Bolivia. I didn't bother with it after that.

We mainly use house-sitting, hostels and AirBnB. I try to allocate $20 a day for accommodation, $20 a day for food and $20 a day for souvenirs, travel and sundries. Our annual cost for everything comes to around $29,000.

Globetrotter Girls (Dani and Jess): f there's one thing we can say about our budget, it is that we are now more confident about spending money. Looking back at our first year, we only spent $28,484 between two people. Back then, being unsure of how to sustain our earnings, we were clearly shoestring travelers. As soon as we were sure this was going to be a lifestyle and not just a 'trip,' we knew we had to start living more comfortably. This meant that, in our second year, spending increased by almost $10,000, coming to $38,152 for two people.

This seems to be our 'comfort zone', and even though it seemed like we were hemorrhaging money traveling through South America in high season, we ended our third year of travel on a similar budget, spending $37,588 between 1 May 2012 and 30 April 2013.

That said, there are some huge difference in how much we spent in each place—in India for example, we spent just over $500 each per month, while in Buenos Aires, Argentina that amount shot up to almost $2,000 per person per month.

John Bardos: Our living costs vary a lot by country. In Thailand, my wife and I can live on $1,200 per month, in Hungary or Turkey it is about $1,600 per month and in Canada or Japan it's about $3,000. How much you fly also influences costs. We typically spend about $4,000 per person on travel costs. Our yearly expenses (for a couple) are less than $25,000 for the last four years including travel costs.

Miller family: We spent $35,000 in 2008 on a 12-month cycle trip through Europe and North Africa for six people. That included airfares, hotels, museums, food and everything else involved in the trip—approximately half of what our annual family budget 'at home' was the year before.

Denning family: We spend $500–$1,000 a month on food for our family of eight, depending on the country. We have very few healthcare costs, except for purchasing things like essential oils, where we spend $100–$200 a month. For accommodations, we've spent anywhere from $250–$1,000 a month (depending on the country). Internet is $30–$80/month. Electricity is usually $50–$150/month. Last year we spent $25,000–$30,000 living in Guatemala, Nicaragua and Costa Rica.

Ryan James: I think our situation was much different than most; we never made a budget for the long haul. We had $10,000 in savings and Ron's pension coming in each month. The plan was to travel for as long as we could, be as frugal as we could, and then return home when we ran out of money. In the beginning, we had no destination in mind; it was a vagabond adventure.

When we decided to stay in Hungary, it was only meant to be for three months before we'd move onward. During that time, we spent $450 a month on rent plus $150 on utilities. Food was dirt cheap; $100 covered our food bill for the month.

Healthwise, both of us were covered by Ron's insurance which cost $550 a month. We now have Hungarian insurance through our business so we dropped the Blue Cross.

Nora Dunn: In 2011, her expenses totaled $17,615 and included five months in New Zealand, two and a half months in Canada and the U.S., two weeks in Sweden, "the ultimate train challenge" (29 trains in 30 days from Portugal to Vietnam), two weeks in Vietnam and two months in Grenada. In 2012, her travelling lifestyle cost $28,032 and included three months sailing the Caribbean, a month in Florida, three months house-sitting in Grenada, two months house-sitting in Switzerland (with time in Paris and London) and three months back in Grenada.

Whatever the cost of traveling and living in other countries, there is often a fear of not having enough money or running out along the way. The Miller family ran out of money while they were on the road in Italy and the Denning family lost a chunk of their savings in the stock market crash while they were in Costa Rica. Both families are still on the road with no intention of returning home.

Caz and Craig Makepeace started a travel blog in 2010 to share their experiences of 16 years of round-the-world travel: living and working in five countries and travelling through 52. In a post about "running out of money," Caz says, "You absolutely could run out of money. But, then again you might not. Why don't you put your energy and thought into the second scenario? Why bet on yourself to fail? If you don't bet on your-self to succeed, who will?"

In their blog, they provide tips and ideas with a number of 'how-tos,' including how to plan diligently and consider the actual costs involved in heading off into the sunset.

"Let's get down to logic and plans—the food your mind likes and a beast that must be tamed," they write. "Here's what to do if you're scared of running out of money on your travels:

1. Research all your costs for your trip diligently: Research the cost of your travel, food, accommodation, transport and tours for the length of time you are going for.

2. Add in *an emergency buffer:* You're worried about unexpected problems arising? Add in an emergency buffer when budget-ing for your travels.

3. Add in *a dream buffer:* What if you arrive at the Great Barrier Reef, but don't have the money to go scuba diving? It's been your dream since you first saw Nemo, and it's one of the reasons you decided to travel in the first place. You know your purpose for travelling; it is about the everyday journey, but it's also about those bucket list moments.

4. List your income: How much money do you need? (travel expenses + emergency buffer + dream buffer). *Where is your*

money coming from? Do you need to work extra hours or a second job in the lead-up to your travels? How can you create more money?

Craig and I always worked extra jobs, extra hours, boarded out rooms in our house, or sold things. How can you *earn money on the road?*

"Make a list of all the things you could possibly do to make money while you're travelling. I've seen people sell homemade jewelry from their vans and stop to work as cleaners and farm-hands in lodges and properties. A friend earned some extra cash travelling by giving haircuts to other travelers in the caravan parks. You could teach yoga or meditation or offer personal train-ing, provide babysitting services, or car tune-ups. Think of all those people travelling who no longer have access to those things you get in a permanent settled life. How can you supply them with what they need and make a bit of cash on the side? I've worked in all kinds of jobs around the world to make money. I even chipped barnacles off pearl shells in the tail end of a cyclone just so I could get the money to travel more.

"It's rare for me to meet anyone who has ever regretted trav-elling, even if they did run out of money. It's also rare for me to meet someone whose life has not been greatly improved because they did travel—whether they ran out of money or not."

There's one more major factor to consider: It's not about the money. A friend recently told us: **"I've heard of plenty of people who've lost their money and got it back again, but I've never heard of anyone who lost time and got it back."**

Resources

The following organizations, books and websites are among those that have been recommended:

Woofing (wwoof.net)
   Worldwide opportunities on organic farms

Warm showers (warmshowers.org)
   Free worldwide hospitality exchange for touring cyclists.

Couchsurfing (couchsurfing.org)
   Free worldwide accommodation in the homes of other people making their rooms (or couches) available to travelers.

RoadScholar (formerly Elderhostel) (roadscholar.org)
   international nonprofit organization offering older adults short-term, low-cost courses, housing, andmeals, usually on college campuses

Workaways - workaway.info

Opportunities to work abroad

Teaching English Overseas

Obtain a TEFL certificate to open the world of teaching abroad and research carefully to find a program whose mission, values and details fit with what you want.

Peace Corps (U.S. only) - peacecorps.gov

Volunteer at grassroots level with this preeminent service organization of the United States.

VSO International - vsointernational.org

International development organisation that works through volunteers to fight poverty in developing countries.

Voluntary Service Overseas (VSO) Great Britain only vso.org.uk

Volunteers in Asia - via-programs.org

Private volunteer organization dedicated to increasing understanding between the United States and Asia through service and education

Books

The Four Hour Work Week—Tim Ferriss

Zen And the Art of Motorcycle Maintenance—Robert M. Pirsig

The Art of Non-Conformity—Chris Guillebeau

The New Global Student—Maya Frost

The Number—Lee Eisenberg

Phra Farang—Peter Robinson

Blue Highways—William Least Heat-Moon

Travels with Charley—John Steinbeck

On The Road—Jack Kerouac

Websites and Blogs

1dad1kid - 1dad1kid.com

  (Talon Windwalker)

JetSetCitizen - jetsetcitizen.com

  (John Bardos)

The Happiness Plunge - happinessplunge.com

  (Adam Pervez)

The Dropout Diaries - thedropoutdiaries.com

  (Barbara Adam)

D Travels 'Round - dtravelsround.com

  (Diana Edelman)

TheProfessionalHobo - theprofessionalhobo.com

  (Nora Dunn)

Budget Nomad - http://budgetnomad.blogspot.com

  (Dr. Ryan James)

Here I Go Again On My Own - hereigoagainonmyown.com

(Ramon Stoppelenburg)

Globetrotter Girls - globetrottergirls.com

(Dani and Jess)

FutureExpatsForum - futureexpats.com

(Susanna Perkins)

DiscoverShareInspire - discovershareinspire.com

(The Denning Family)

YOLO ! MomOnTheGo - yolomomonthego.wordpress.com

(Roseariet Swagemakers)

BohemianTravelers - bohemiantravelers.com

(Mary, Jeff and sons)

The Edventure Project - edventureproject.com

(Miller family)

International Cravings - internationalcravings.com

(Chentnik family)

A King's Life - akingslife.com

(King family)

Family On Bikes - familyonbikes.org

(Nancy Sathre-Vogel)

That Life - thatlife.com

(Jim Trick)

YTravel - ytravelblog.com

(Caz and Craig Makepeace)

Additional Websites

Our Travel Lifestyle - ourtravellifestyle.com

(The Burns family)

Escape Artistes - escapeartistes.com

(Theodora and Son)

Twenty-Something Travel - twenty-somethingtravel.com

(Stephanie Yoder)

Escape Artist - escapeartist.com

(an excellent source for information, resources, analysis and insights for the international expat community)

Mindmyhouse.com

Member-based website introducing people looking for house sitters to travelers looking for houses to mind. (We are members of this service and use it often.)

Trustedhousesitters.com

Member-based website introducing people looking for house sitters to travelers looking for houses to mind. (We are members of this service and use it often.)

Housecarers.com

Member-based website introducing people looking for house sitters to travelers looking for houses to mind. (We are not members of this service, for no apparent reason other than the fact that two services is more than enough for our needs.)

Acknowledgements

We wish to acknowledge the following people and places for their love, support, encouragement and inspiration in helping not only make this book happen, but for playing integral roles in our changing attitudes and lifestyle:

Thanks to our talented group of friends/editors who provided us with insights and reactions to our early draft. Tim Lundergan, Susan Spencer, Bob Powell and Sheila Consaul-your wisdom and guidance proved essential as we worked to hone the initial product and come up with something worthwhile.

Hats off and thank you to the families and individuals who responded to our initial survey more than two years ago and endured our endless follow-up questions. Your stories form the backbone of this book (Section Two—Stories from the Other Side of Convention), and give credibility and breadth of experience to the idea of breaking free and creating new lives. Your tales are heartwarming, informative and inspirational.

We wrote this book at a snail's pace over three-and-a-half years, spending hours in coffee shops, hotels, restaurants and other odd places—wherever we could find Wi-Fi—as we wound our way through Southeast Asia and into India, China, Europe and into South America. Here's a partial listing of places that tolerated our presence as we nursed a coffee or a cold drink and researched and wrote away the hours:

Java Cafe, Blue Pumpkin and Brown Coffee, Phnom Penh, Cambodia.

Atomic Coffee, Marblehead, Mass.

Cafe de Jack, Lijaing, China

Cafe Hood, Banos, Ecuador

Costa Coffee, Larnaca, Cyprus

Elmer's Store, Ashfield, Mass.

Gulu Gulu Cafe, Salem, Mass.

Cafe Nucallacta, Cuenca, Ecuador

Corozones Cafe, Ollantaytambo, Peru

Cusco Coffee Company, Arequipa, Peru

Dreams Hotel, Arequipa, Peru

Starbucks, Arequipa, Peru

Rancho Viejo, Cieneguilla, Peru

Other locations offered hotels, coffee shops and house sits where we broke out our laptops and banged away:

Hanoi, Vietnam

Bangkok, Thailand

Ho Chi Minh City, Vietnam

Crowborough, England

Lewes, England

London, England

Haarlem, The Netherlands

Katchanaburi, Thailand

Pattaya, Thailand

Plaisians, France

Gaucin, Spain

San Casciano, Italy

Thanks to Kirsty and Emily Yetter, Skip's daughters, who celebrated our exodus with joy and excitement and joined us along the way to partake in some of life's magic on the road. Without their love and support, none of this would have been possible.

Thank you to Colette Said—Gabi's mum—who imbued her daughter with an unquenchable spirit of adventure and a zest for life that is beyond compelling.

Last but certainly not least, props to our intrepid editor and designer Dave Bricker, whose gentle coaxing, deft editing hand and keen sense of humor made this project a whole lot better—and fun.

Countless other family members and friends played parts in our ongoing adventure. You know who you are. We love you and value you.

CPSIA information can be obtained at www.ICGtesting.com
Printed in the USA
BVOW02s2353270915

419299BV00006B/156/P